ANTONY ATHA

TIPS

FOR THE lazy GARDENER

ANTONY ATHA

TIPS

FOR THE lazy GARDENER

GRAMERCY

CONTENTS

Photography © Collins and Brown

Publisher: Lisa Simpson
Designer: Emily Cook
Picture researcher: Sarah Epton

© 2000 by Parkgate Books Limited

This 2001 edition is published by Gramercy Books™,
an imprint of Random House Value Publishing. Inc.,
280 Park Avenue, New York, NY 10017.
by arrangement with Parkgate Books Limited,
London House, Great Eastern Wharf, Parkgate Road, London, SW11 4NQ

Gramercy Books™ and design are registered trademarks of
Random House Value Publishing

Random House
New York • Toronto • London • Sydney • Auckland
http://www.randomhouse.com/

A CIP catalogue record for this book is available from the Library of Congress

ISBN 0-517-16319-5

PRINTED AND BOUND IN CHINA

8 7 6 5 4 3 2 1

TIPS FOR THE lazy GARDENER

INTRODUCTION

There is no such thing as a beautiful garden that requires no work at all. There are many people who enjoy gardening enormously and relish the effort and the time spent out of doors. They get great satisfaction from seeing plants bloom, and planting and harvesting the fresh vegetables from the kitchen garden. But there are many others who either do not want to spend hours gardening, or who cannot afford the time because of other pressures and demands.

This book is written for them. In a sense it is quite hard work being a lazy gardener, you have to plan quite carefully, you have to know the type of plants that will grow happily in the conditions that you can offer them, and you have to decide exactly what your priorities are, and stick to them if you possibly can. As an example it is no good in the summer thinking that you are going to be a lazy gardener and mow the lawn every two weeks rather than once a week. Grass grows quickly. If you cut it every two weeks it will take you more than twice as long to mow it, and the lawn will not be nearly so healthy. If you have a lawn and you are unable to cut it regularly the best advice is to try and find someone who will cut the grass for you. Then the garden will, at least, look reasonably tidy.

Many people are faced with a garden that exists when they move into a new house. If you are confronted by a garden that requires a large amount of work, can only devote a small amount of time to looking after it, and you want the garden to look reasonably presentable, there is a number of things that you can do to lessen the work load. First of all count the number of different elements in the garden. How many different patches of grass, flower beds, herbaceous borders, shrubberies are there, is there a kitchen garden that is either separate, or an integral part of the existing garden design? Each element requires a certain number of man or woman hours throughout the year to maintain it properly, relatively weed-free, and the flowers and shrubs blooming at the correct time of year. Reducing the number of elements means lessening the time you have to spend.

Can you do without the vegetable garden? Growing vegetables takes a lot of time and effort and if you put it down to grass, and mow it, this requires far, far, fewer hours over the course of the year. Can you get

Left: A summer arrangement of annuals in shades of pink and purple. Pink petunias are planted with pansies, argyranthemum and cineraria.

7

rid of one or two of the existing beds? If you can you may be able to grass them over too. What plants do you have in the beds? If you have suitable acid soil, and are not too fussy, you could consider replacing a flower bed with a bed of heathers interspersed with dwarf conifers. Once established this will require relatively little work and provide good color in the winter.

Alternatively, if you want to retain a border, can you introduce more shrubs that require less attention during the summer? It is perfectly possible to plan a mixed shrub and perennial border that needs less work than a herbaceous border. If you want instant color, and the border is not too large, you could dig up a mixed border and replace it with annual bedding plants that you can change with the seasons. Winter pansies will provide color in the winter months and a bed of traditional annuals will provide color throughout the summer. These can be bought from the local garden center or nursery and planted out in position to give you instant color. You will need to dig up the plants each season and plant the new ones and control the weeds but this is less work than tending a traditional herbaceous border.

Right: *Erigeron glaucus*.

THE LAWN

8

The first thing that the lazy gardener has to consider is whether he or she can do without a lawn altogether. If you live in a town and your garden is not too large then this is perfectly possible. You can replace the lawn with a paved area – paving is available in a number of finishes, some of which are extremely attractive – or, if your garden is too large for this, you can consider putting the lawn area down to gravel. This is a much cheaper alternative and something favored by many of the most fashionable garden designers. If you are going to put the lawn, or any area, down to gravel it is a good idea to level it first and then apply weedkiller to the whole surface. If you want this area to be permanent lay thick black plastic sheets or old carpet over it and then cover the top with a good layer of gravel. This will help to exclude the weeds.

If you have a garden where there is a lawn and the garden is too large to get rid of it, then the first thing the lazy gardener has to do is ensure that he or she has a lawnmower that will cut it quickly and efficiently. If you have a smallish square in a town you may well get away with a hover-mower, but anything larger is much easier to care for with a wheeled rotary mower equipped with a grass collection box. There are many good models available. If you have a garden with a serious amount of grass, and you still have aspirations to be a lazy gardener, then you must get a ride-on mower capable of cutting half an acre or so of grass within 30 minutes. These are expensive machines but if you plan to be lazy, you have to pay for the privilege.

Another thing to consider as a possibility is to let some of the garden go to rough grass. This might well suit a large informal garden in the country, especially areas such as old orchards. You will still need to cut the grass once or twice a year and clear it up (or get someone to make hay for you if the grass is cut at the correct time). A simpler solution to this problem might be to keep geese, goats or sheep, who will graze the grass for you, although goats and sheep will eat trees and shrubs as well as grass.

It is always possible to mow paths through rough areas of grass and these can provide pleasant walkways through the garden. Whatever you do, if you are a lazy gardener, do not be tempted to convert any part of the garden to a wildflower meadow. This is a very difficult thing to accomplish successfully, far more difficult than planting and maintaining a herbaceous border, and harder work.

Looking after lawns requires

some thought and you have to decide how much time and effort you are prepared to devote to the grass. For most people, as long as the lawn is reasonably well mown, that is all they are looking for. Mow the lawn once a week during the summer, except possibly in late spring or early summer when the grass grows very quickly and you might need to mow every four or five days. Whatever you do don't be tempted to cut the grass too short. Leave the cutters reasonably high all summer and the lawn will stay greener and the grass will grow better as a result.

If you want to eliminate some of the weeds then you can apply a specific weedkiller that will kill all broad-leaved plants in the lawn, such as dandelion and plantain, leaving you with the grass. If you have a lot of moss in the lawn you can consider applying lawn sand to kill this off in the spring, although one of the advantages of a mossy lawn is that it remains reasonably green even in a very dry summer. When the moss is dead, it really should be raked out as this gives the grass more room and air that it needs to flourish.

If you decide that you want to be a lazy gardener no longer, then you can hire equipment in the early spring to pull out the long roots of grass and break up the topsoil. Within six or seven weeks, the whole lawn will be healthier and will therefore grow better.

Opposite: Curved edges in a lawn create a feeling of informality in a garden. It is important to clip the edges every time you mow.

Left top: Sunshine and shade emphasise the attractions of a formal lawn.

Left bottom: A broad grass path separates two formal beds in a narrow garden.

9

SHRUBS
FOR LOW MAINTENANCE

Above: *Cornus alba* 'Sibirica Variegata' is a popular shrub with variegated leaves and red stems in the winter.

Below and opposite: Sprays of the fragrant *Viburnum tinus,* laurustinus. This shrub should be grown in all gardens.

Opposite bottom: *Heliotropium arborescens* 'Marine'. Heliotropes are only half-hardy and often grown as annuals

Shrubs are an excellent way to add color and form to your garden. They are pretty low maintenance and require relatively little work from the lazy gardener. The problems can really be boiled down to which shrubs to choose and here it pays to be very careful and to learn about each shrub as otherwise you may well be disappointed.

As a general rule most shrubs flower in spring or early summer. If you only grow shrubs then your garden might look a bit plain in late summer and fall. There are, however, a number of shrubs that flower in all months of the year and by careful choice the lazy gardener can always have some in flower.

REQUIREMENTS
Check carefully the requirements of the shrub that you plan to plant and the soil and conditions that are present in your garden. If you live in areas where the weather tends to be dry, the soil alkaline, and it is often quite cold in the winter, you will not really be able to grow rhododendrons or azaleas successfully as they generally like warmth, rain, and acid soil. There are many shrubs that prefer slightly acid soil and it really pays to check before buying; however attractive you may think a plant is, it will not always be suited to your soil type.

Another easy-to-follow tip is to check the gardens of your neighbors. What are they growing that looks well, happy and attractive? Even if you cannot recognise the shrub yourself, they will know and you will find one in a local nursery. Plants that flourish locally are the ones for the lazy gardener to concentrate on.

SIZE AND VIGOR
It is important to check, at the time you buy, on the ultimate size of the plant you plan to purchase. You may live in a small town garden and be very fond of ceanothus with their wonderful chalk-blue flowers of late spring. Ceanothus will probably flourish brilliantly in the warm conditions that many town gardens provide but many varieties are pretty vigorous and may well outgrow their allotted space within a few short years. Even hard cutting back will not keep them in bounds. This principle applies to a number of shrubs and a quick check, either with a knowledgeable nurseryman, or in a gardening encyclopedia, will save you having to cut down and dig out some favorite plant because it has grown too big for the garden.

This principle applies to any garden no matter what the size. Certain vigorous plants should really be avoided altogether, such as x *Cupressocyparis leylandii*. It grows into a large hedge very quickly, but to keep it within bounds you need to clip it three or four times a year, and it has caused endless trouble with neighbors when it has been planted as a hedge in relatively small gardens. Other, better, more

amenable hedging plants exist. Also never grow the Russian vine, now correctly called *Fallopia baldschuanica*, formerly *Polygonum baldschuanicum*, under which name it can still be found in nurseries. It grows far too fast and is both deciduous and uncontrollable; nor, really the lovely clary, *Salvia sclarea* var. *turkestanica*, in the herbaceous border, it seeds itself so prolifically that you will find it can take over the whole border within the space of three or four years.

BUYING

When you have decided on the type of shrubs and trees that you want to grow in your garden then you have to set about acquiring them. Generally speaking, leaving aside any keen and expert friends who might give you some plants they have grown as cuttings, there are three places where you can go to buy plants. All have advantages and disadvantages.

Above: The beautiful dahlia 'Bishop of Llandaff'.

Opposite: Choosing plants in a garden center.

MAIL ORDER BARGAIN OFFERS

These are an extension of the mail order principle but should be treated with some caution. ADVANTAGES: they are cheap; they are a good way of filling a large bare garden quickly and cheaply with common varieties. DISADVANTAGES: the plants may not be what you expect; you may have difficulty obtaining redress should this be necessary; the descriptions of the plants are generally pretty glowing, possibly rather too glowing; the choice is limited.

THE GARDEN CENTER

The most convenient is your local garden center or nursery. ADVANTAGES: you can see what you are buying – this is a great help to the beginner-gardener who may not know exactly what the plant looks like in flower; you can take the plants home with you then and there; you can check on the condition of the plant. DISADVANTAGES: the choice is often limited to the more popular varieties; the plants are nearly always container-grown; they are often only available for sale when they are in flower; container-grown plants are often rather expensive.

MAIL-ORDER NURSERY

The next easiest place to buy plants is from a mail-order nursery. ADVANTAGES: the plants can be chosen carefully from the catalogue and you can check there and then on the dimensions and requirements to make sure that the plant is correct for your garden; the range available is wide; reputable mail order suppliers have a country-wide reputation and many firms will refund the cost of the plant if it dies within a year; plants are generally cheaper than those available in the local garden center. DISADVANTAGES: you cannot see what you are buying; the plants are usually a bit smaller than you expect; they are sent via post or carrier so may arrive at an inconvenient moment and have to be dealt with straight away; shrubs and trees supplied as bare-root specimens have to be heeled in if you cannot plant them when they arrive.

SUPERMARKETS AND OTHER HIGH STREET STORES

Many large shopping outlets stock pre-packaged plants and trees during the growing season.

ADVANTAGES: they are often seriously cheap compared with other outlets.

DISADVANTAGES: the choice is minimal; shops are poor places to keep plants and they may well have deteriorated in condition; no knowledgeable help will be available.

However if you buy at the beginning of the planting season and only want common varieties this can be a good, cheap way to stock a garden.

There is really no such thing as a 'bargain' when buying plants with the exception of the end-of-year container-grown shrub or tree in good condition that is being sold off cheaply as it is past its flowering stage. The only trouble about this is that you have to know what the shrub is and looks like in flower to be able to buy successfully.

PLANTING
AND PRUNING

Plants are sold in three ways: growing in a container; bare-root i.e. dug up by a mail-order nursery and supplied with damp material, such as peat, around the roots – pre-packaged plants are also supplied in this condition; balled plants, generally conifers that are often dug up with the root ball intact and supplied with the soil around the roots wrapped in a ball of sacking.

Contrary to what you might expect, plants purchased as bare-root specimens and planted in the right way have a better chance of making good plants than most container-grown specimens. This applies particularly to roses.

PLANTING BARE-ROOT AND PRE-PACKAGED PLANTS
The plant
If you can, plant new plants within 2 or 3 days of their arrival, leave them wrapped up with the damp peat packed around their roots in a dry, frost-free place and check that the roots are moist. Water if necessary. If they have to be left for longer then they should be heeled in. Dig a trench in the garden, lay the plants in the trench leaning against one side and then fill the trench in. Tread the soil to firm it.

When you are ready to plant, unpack the plants carefully or remove them from the trench, and stand them in a bucket of water for 2 hours. Examine the roots and trim any damaged roots or any that are

too long. After planting check that the plant is firm in the hole and trim off any thin weak shoots or old leaves and flowers. If you are planting bare-root plants in the spring, and they have started into growth, cut back the shoots by half so that the root system does not have to support too many leaves and buds before it has become established.

The hole
Prepare a planting mix of 1 part topsoil, 1 part peat or good garden compost, 2 handfuls of either bonemeal, fish blood and bone per barrowload.
Warning: if you live in a suburban area do not add either bonemeal or fish blood and bone to any newly planted shrub. Any urban rodent will think that a delicious smelly fish lies at the bottom of your hole and will uproot the shrub time after time, use fertilizer instead.

Alternatively, for the lazy gardener, mix in some garden compost with the topsoil when you dig the planting hole for the new shrub and scatter some fertilizer at the bottom of the hole.

Dig out a good hole and see that the subsoil or pan is broken up. If this is not done then the roots of the plant may be unable to penetrate into the subsoil. It is important that the hole is wide enough to accommodate the plant easily. If you are planting a tree or shrub in a lawn then dig a square hole, not a circle – squares are much easier to keep tidy and mow

around – remove the turf to the compost heap, and make sure that the area is about twice as large as you think is really necessary. You will be surprised how quickly shrubs outgrow their allotted space.

Check the level of the plant and refill the hole with planting mixture so that plant rests in the hole and the soil level matches the old soil mark on its stem. Add some trowelfuls of planting mixture and push this around the roots with your fingers. Cover up all the roots, pushing the soil down to eliminate any possible air pockets and then tread it firm. Fill the planting hole with planting mixture, tread the soil down again and then loosen the topsoil slightly with a garden fork, water well and then cover with a good layer of mulch.

These basic instructions apply to all planting and it is worthwhile taking care to plant new shrubs and trees properly as you will then have less trouble with them and they are more likely to flourish.

PLANTING IN THE SUMMER MONTHS

Gardening books and writers always assume that you will only plant at the ideal time of the year, in the fall or in early spring. Very often, however, even the lazy gardener has to move a plant or shrub in high summer. If you do this, make sure you water the plant thoroughly before moving it, and then that the plant is 'puddled in' and the hole and ground are really wet in the new position.

Generally, if care is taken, the plant will survive perfectly. Check on the plant daily and keep it watered in dry periods.

PLANTING CONTAINER-GROWN AND BALLED SPECIMENS

Make sure that your planting hole is large enough for the container to be surrounded by at least 7.5–10 cm (3–4 in) of planting mixture in all directions, including underneath. Water the container well. If you can, place the plant in the hole and carefully cut away the plastic or sacking around the roots. Examine the roots and tease out any that are tangled or circling. Fill around the plant with planting mix, peat, or peat substitute. Even if you are the laziest of lazy gardeners, don't just refill your hole with ordinary soil when planting container-grown plants, as their roots may well not grow out of the compost in the container into the surrounding soil.

If you are planting a plant growing in a solid plastic container lay it on its side and give the rim a sharp tap. This will usually be enough to loosen the plant but if the roots have grown through the drainage holes at the bottom of the container you may well have to cut them away. Try and keep the soil ball around the roots as intact as you can.

PLANTING TREES

It is a good idea to stake any trees you plant. If you are planting bare-root trees drive in the stake before you

Opposite top: If you are planting a container-grown shrub in dry weather in summer it is essential to water the ground thoroughly and and 'puddle' the plant in.

Opposite bottom: Check the level of the plant against the soil level and fill in the hole so that the plant rests on the planting mix. Fill in around the plant and water again.

plant the tree; off center in your planting hole and on the side of the prevailing wind, southwest, in most gardens. If you are planting a container-grown tree drive the stake in sideways at a 45° angle on the side away from the prevailing wind.

PRUNING

Pruning causes more worry and controversy than anything else in the garden. Many shrubs and trees are better for pruning and any pruning must be carried out at the right time of the year although many shrubs will survive unpruned for several seasons. The lazy gardener concentrates on growing those shrubs. If you are in doubt about how and when a shrub should be pruned check in a specialist pruning manual.

There may well be some trees and shrubs that have to be pruned in your garden already. These may include:

Hybrid tea, floribunda and patio roses

Cut them straight through about 45 cm (18 in) above ground. Remove any dead wood down to the ground.

Climbers, ramblers and shrub roses

These should be pruned after flowering in the fall. Consult a specialist book on pruning for details. Ramblers are awkward to prune.

Hedges

These have to be trimmed regularly as otherwise they grow too tall, and also too thin as the bottom grows out of them. If you are a lazy gardener and have to plant a hedge don't plant privet, lawsoniana, or box as they have to be trimmed two or three times a year.

Shrubs that need pruning

Vigorous shrubs that flower on new wood each year: these include fuchsias, *Buddleja davidii*, *Cornus alba* (for its stems), mallow (lavatera) and Cape figwort (phygelius). Cut all these down pretty well to the ground in early spring. If you do not do this then the plant will become leggy and produce fewer and fewer flowers.

There is a number of other spring and early summer-flowering shrubs that should be pruned after flowering, such as philadelphus and weigela. This encourages the new growth that will carry next year's flowers. However, you do not absolutely have to prune these. Judge whether the plant is growing in the right way and prune accordingly. If you are in doubt consult a pruning manual.

Finally you may want to cut back a shrub that has outgrown its allotted space in the garden. If you can bear it, do this over a three-year period, removing one-third of the main stems each spring. If you have a really large hedge or bank of plants that need to be reduced in size, laurels are an example that springs to mind, cut one half of the hedge right down on one side, wait for five years when new growth will have got going and then take the other half down.

Opposite: Cutting a floribunda rose for an indoor flower arrangement. It is a good idea to deadhead all roses as this conserves the strength of the plant. The only exception is roses grown for the size and color of their hips in the fall. These include *Rosa* 'Hibernica', a variety of the common dog rose, and *R. moyesii* and its varieties.

17

GARDENING ESSENTIALS

1
CLAY

2
PEAT

3
LOAM SOIL

4
SANDY SOIL

YOUR SOIL

It is important to test your soil to find out how acid or alkaline it is. Some plants prefer one condition, some the other. The ideal soil has a neutral pH of 6.5–7. If you purchase a simple soil-testing kit and follow the instructions this will show you the acidity or otherwise of the soil in your garden. This has a direct effect on the plants that will flourish there. Even a lazy gardener needs to find out the soil type for otherwise you may find yourself trying to grow plants that will not thrive in your garden: soils are classified as loamy (the best) and then clay, sandy, chalky, peaty or stony, or some combination of these. Peaty soil is almost invariably acid, but clay soil may be either acid or alkaline.

THE ASPECT OF YOUR GARDEN

You also have to consider the aspect of the garden. Is it sheltered or open to the winds? Does the prevailing wind affect it? Which direction does it face, north, south, east or west? Is it directly in the sun for most of the day or, if you live in a town, is the garden shaded for much of the time? There are plants that will flourish in shade and don't like too much sun and, again, it makes sense to concentrate on those plants that will grow well in the conditions that you can offer them.

All this requires thought, care and study. All the information is available in gardening magazines and books and, failing those, good practical advice can usually be obtained from knowledgeable neighbors.

19

Left: An old-fashioned garden border in full growth in summer. Note how the grey and silver shrubs help to divide up the blocks of color and the purple-pink flowers of *Allium giganteum,* the ornamental onion, form a focal point.

COMPOST

DON'T

A major don't is to add weeds. Bag them up and take them to the local dump or make a separate heap if you have room and burn them.

Even the laziest of lazy gardeners should make an attempt to make some compost. The amount you make depends very much on the size of your garden and the amount of suitable material it produces. Most gardening books give precise instructions on how to make the best compost and in an ideal world they should be followed with care. There are three main elements produced by most gardens that can be used for compost. These are grass clippings, leaves that drop in the fall and kitchen waste (potato peelings etc, not plastic), plus cardboard or newspaper.

grass clippings cardboard
leaves
kitchen waste
potato peelings newspaper

RULES

Make as large a heap as you can.

Confine it in some way, a wire netting cage or some garden trellis works well. Contrary to what you sometimes read compost needs some air.

Add grass clippings throughout the summer, as well as kitchen waste and torn up cardboard or newspaper. Add them in layers if you can. If you can't, don't bother.

Leave the compost heap open to the air as it benefits from some moisture, also most compost heaps are under trees or placed innocuously in the corners of gardens sheltered by walls but many recommend that it is covered with old carpet. The idea is to get the heap as hot as possible and then turn it over so that the material degrades at an even rate.

When the leaves start to drop in the fall collect them with a rotary mower, or put them through a shredder, and add them to the heap. Turn them over as much as possible and keep piling up the heap through the winter.

A heap completed at the end of the fall will be composted in twelve to fifteen months, brown, crumbly and beautiful. Dig it away so that you start using the oldest, bottom right-hand corner first, so to speak, and you can repeat this simple process without activators, or earth, or much effort each year.

Professional compost makers will say that this is incorrect, it should be done much more carefully and you can make better compost in six to eight months. This may well be true but this way is very satisfactory for the lazy gardener.

Of course you can add other material such as shredded chippings if you have a shredder but such machines are not really for the lazy gardener. If you come across any material that has not composted properly, probably leaves or long grass as they take longest, just shift them across to the heap you are constructing the following year.

21

WEEDS

Weed control is part of gardening and the lazy gardener must try to lessen the time spent weeding. There are two ways of controlling weeds, apart from getting down on your hands and knees and removing annual weeds with a fork. The first is to reduce the area they can colonise. Grow ground-cover plants in the border, cover borders with mulch (this smothers a number of weeds and the ones that survive are far more easily removed), lay barriers of plastic or newspaper and cover them with compost or gravel. All these measures help to reduce the number of weeds in the garden. The other way is to use chemical control and a certain amount of chemical control is usually needed, however green your intentions may be. Most gardeners use a combination of these two methods.

Warning: be very careful about the weather conditions when you apply weedkillers and check the manufacturer's instructions carefully. Never, ever, apply weedkiller by spray on a windy day as it will be blown on to other plants and kill them just as surely as it kills the weeds. Spray very carefully to reduce the possibility of drift. Never apply a systemic weedkiller (one that works through the foliage down to the roots of the plant) or any

herbicide in the middle of a very hot fine day in midsummer. They will evaporate before they have had time to take effect.

Certain areas of the garden should be treated with weedkiller as a matter of course. The first place is a gravel drive and any path. Apply one of the weedkillers formulated to prevent weeds growing early in spring before weed growth starts and again in late summer when the effect starts to wear off.

KITCHEN GARDEN AND BORDERS

You can prevent the emergence of annual surface weeds by treating areas of the garden with a pre-emergent granular weedkiller. This will not harm any established woody plants but it creates a chemical cap on the soil that prevents annual surface weeds germinating. These weedkillers are based on the chemical dichlobenil.

Certain weeds must be treated chemically as no amount of hoeing (not a pursuit for the lazy gardener), digging out, mulching or any other method will work. Chief among them is bindweed – couch grass and creeping thistle are other candidates. Systemic weedkillers that work down to the roots of the plants based on glyphosate are the most effective, readily available and easy to use. These weedkillers will not harm the soil and you can

Opposite: Some perennial weeds, such as dandelions, have long tap roots. Try to remove the whole root using a special long-bladed prong or narrow trowel.

Left: Apply systemic weedkillers on cool days when there is little wind. Follow the instructions carefully and wear a protective mask and clothing.

cultivate immediately, once the plants have died. However they do take some time to work and more than one application may be necessary before the weed dies.

The other main weedkillers are based on paraquat. These burn off all green foliage they come in contact with and become inactive immediately they come in contact with the soil. They will not rid the garden of any persistent weeds on a permanent basis.

Other weeds can gradually be eliminated by mowing or cutting down. Nettles are one of the weeds that doesn't like being cut down regularly, ground elder is another.

TOOLS

All gardeners, lazy or otherwise, are advised to buy the best garden tools that they can afford and to have as large a range of tools available as possible. This may be a counsel of perfection but it can save a great deal of time, worry and effort.

Don't forget that you will need tools such as, a hammer, wire cutters, nails, and screwdrivers as well as the conventional gardening equipment.

24

ESSENTIAL TOOLS
Lawnmowers
Buy a lawnmower that will enable you to cut all your grass as quickly as possible, however expensive. Also, for the novice gardener, buy a rotary mower rather than a cylinder mower and if you want rolled stripes on the lawn, buy a model that has a roller on the back and not just wheels. Buy a mower that collects the grass, not only will the lawn look better and be healthier, but you will provide yourself with the basic ingredient for garden compost.

Forks, spades, rakes, hoes
You will need at least one of each. It is useful to have a flat plastic rake to rake up leaves as well as a traditional rake that you will need if you have to prepare beds for sowing vegetables in the kitchen garden, a lawn rake with springed tines for raking moss from the lawn or raking gravel is also useful. Stainless steel spades make digging easier but they have very sharp edges and slice open the bottoms of gumboots with effortless ease.

Trowels, hand forks, weeders
You will need one of each. It can help to have two trowels, one with a broad blade, one with a narrow one.

Pruning tools
You will need one good pair of shears, possibly a pair of trimmers although these may not be essential in a small garden, a pruning saw, and a gardening knife.

Shears
You will need a pair of edging shears to keep the lawn edges neat, and a pair of ordinary shears to clip hedges of plants such as lavender.

Wheelbarrow
Buy as big a wheelbarrow as you need and get one with a proper tire at the front. It is much easier to push when it is full of heavy soil.

Watering cans and sprayers
You really should have two watering cans, one for beneficial watering, one reserved for weedkilling only. You also need a sprayer to spray roses and other plants in the summer, ideally you should have two of these, but if you make do with one wash it out thoroughly after use.

NON-ESSENTIAL TOOLS
There is a number of other tools that you may, or may not, be able to survive without. These include: bulb planters, worth having if you plant a lot of bulbs; dibbers, essential really if you are planting out leeks in the garden; cultivating tools, they can be quite useful but you can get by with a fork and rake; aerators for the lawn, you can make do with a fork but it isn't quite as good or quick; half-moon edgers, they make a better job of edging a lawn than the slightly

curved spade; leaf sweepers; hosepipes and sprinklers, pretty essential really – you can invest as much money as you can afford on sophisticated computer-controlled irrigation systems if you want, but a hose and sprinkler head is usually enough; garden lines, for sowing seeds in a straight line; nylon linc trimmers; hedgecutters; chipper/shredder machines; axe, pickaxe; sledgehammer; rotary cultivator; chainsaw; long armed tree pruner.

Many of these tools are a great help if you have a large garden and not much manual assistance.

If you become fired with enthusiasm and cease to be a lazy gardener you will also need seed trays, pots and modular systems. These are all a help when sowing seeds under glass.

Left: Always buy the best gardening tools you can afford and clean them properly after use. Parrot-beak shears and a large wheelbarrow with an inflatable front tire are specifically recommended. The French spade shown in the collection of tools is becoming increasingly popular and is most useful when digging heavy soils.

25

PLANT DIRECTORY

27

Left: Annuals planted in
containers ready to move
into the garden for the
summer. These include
trailing pelargoniums,
marigolds, stocks, lilies and
tobacco plants.

Many popular shrubs will grow easily in most gardens and provide flowers throughout the year. The selections listed below are all readily available and have no specific cultivation requirements.

Aucuba japonica

A hardy evergreen shrub that tolerates shade, poor soil, drought, pollution and salt winds. They have small reddish, insignificant flowers in spring, and the female plants have red berries in the fall if they are grown together with a male plant. The variety *A. j.* 'Crotonifolia' has yellow-speckled leaves. They can be used as a hedge or a specimen plant, are fairly slow-growing, but will eventually reach a height and spread of 4 m (12 ft).
DISADVANTAGES: rather dull.

Berberis darwinii

(Darwin's barberry)
There are many varieties of berberis. *B. darwinii* is a hardy, evergreen species, that has a profusion of orange-yellow flowers in mid to late spring and glossy dark green leaves with three spiky points. The shrub carries small black-blue fruits in the fall. It prefers well-drained moist soil and full sun. It has an upright growth habit, can be grown as a hedge and will reach 3 m (10 ft). Trim after flowering if required.
DISADVANTAGES: slightly sparse habit, prickles.

Chaenomeles japonica

(Japonica, Japanese quince)
A slow-growing, hardy, spreading shrub, usually grown against a wall, that has colorful orange-red flowers in early spring followed by yellow quince fruits in the fall.
C. speciosa is faster growing and has a number of varieties with different colored flowers. All chaenomeles prefer well-drained soil and full sun but will tolerate some shade. If they are grown against a wall they need pruning after flowering to maintain their shape and the shoots need to be tied in. They can reach 1 m (3 ft) in height by 2 m (6 ft) wide.
DISADVANTAGES: prickly spines, needs to be pruned and tied in.

Choisya ternata

(Mexican orange blossom)
A hardy evergreen shrub that will grow well in shade in spite of what many gardening books say. It has clusters of small, white, scented flowers in late spring. It prefers fertile, well-drained soil but tolerates both chalk and clay. The variety 'Sundance' has yellow leaves when grown in the sun. It can reach 1.8 m (6 ft) or more. DISADVANTAGES: fairly vigorous, not for very small gardens.

Cornus alba 'Elegantissima'

(Red-barked dogwood)
One of a large group of favorite garden trees and shrubs that prefer slightly acid soil but will grow well in any soil that is not too alkaline.
Cornus alba 'Elegantissima' is a

hardy deciduous shrub with dark red branches in winter and small clusters of white flowers in spring with elegant grey-green leaves with white margins. It can be left unpruned. *C. a.* 'Sibirica' is generally cut down hard every spring as this promotes the growth of many young, brilliant red shoots for the following winter. Fairly slow-growing, it will reach a height and spread of 3 m (10 ft). DISADVANTAGES: none.

Daphne mezereum
(Mezereon)
A popular, small, upright, deciduous shrub that carries spikes of purple-red, very fragrant flowers from late winter onwards. It likes some protection and moist humus-rich, well-drained soil. It resents being moved, so plant container-grown specimens and it also dislikes being pruned, so confine pruning to removing damaged wood. *D. odora* is evergreen. It will reach 1.2 m (4 ft) in height. DISADVANTAGES: none.

Escallonia 'Apple Blossom'
Escallonias are mostly evergreen but are better grown against a wall in the colder north. In the warmer parts of the country they are often planted as hedges and grow in any reasonable garden soil, chalk or clay, in sun or partial shade. They have masses of small flowers for a long period in summer. The hybrids are the ones usually planted, 'Apple Blossom' has pink and white flowers, 'C.F. Ball', red and *E. rubra* 'Crimson Spire',

29

Opposite: *Chaenomeles* x *superba* carries large clusters of flowers on bare branches in spring followed by quince-like fruits in the fall.

Left top: *Daphne mezereum* has many small tubular pink to purple flowers in late winter and early spring. It is very fragrant.

Left bottom: *Potentilla fruticosa* 'Primrose Beauty'. Potentillas come in a variety of colors from yellow through to pink and orange and flower from late spring through to the fall.

crimson. Trim hedges in the fall. Height and width 2.5 m (8 ft). DISADVANTAGES: better not grown in a very cold or exposed garden.

Elaeagnus pungens 'Maculata'

A hardy evergreen shrub grown entirely for its dark green and yellow strongly marked foliage. It also has small, white, fragrant flowers in spring but they are fairly insignificant. Easy to grow, not too vigorous, it tolerates sun and shade and most garden soils. It does not need pruning and will reach 3 m (10 ft) with a slightly greater spread. DISADVANTAGES: none, providing you like the yellow and green leaves.

Forsythia suspensa

Not quite a lazy gardener shrub but worth considering for the impact of the vivid yellow flowers in early spring each year. Forsythias are deciduous shrubs that will grow in most garden soils and while they do best in full sun, they will also flourish in partial shade. They have a lanky, arching, rather untidy, habit and may need tying in against a wall. If you need to control them they must be pruned immediately flowering is over. Trim back any shoots that have born flowers by a half and every few years cut out some of the mature shoots completely. If you delay you will get a lot of growth and few flowers the following year. Reaches a height of 2.5 m (8 ft). DISADVANTAGES: birds

may peck off the flower buds, care needed over pruning.

Mahonia japonica

An excellent, hardy, evergreen shrub with scented yellow flowers in midwinter. *Mahonia x media* 'Charity' is another excellent variety. Mahonias will grown in any soil in sun or shade and tolerate dry conditions. No pruning is necessary but any unwanted growth can be cut back in spring. Height 1.8 m (6 ft) or more. DISADVANTAGES: none, except the slightly spiky leaves.

Osmanthus delavayi

A slow-growing evergreen shrub with small, white, fragrant flowers in late spring. It will grow in any well-drained garden soil in sun or shade but dislikes cold winds so generally prefers a sheltered position. No pruning is necessary and it reaches 1.5 m (5 ft). DISADVANTAGES: needs some shelter in cold winters.

Potentilla fruticosa

A most useful small shrub that is in flower from late spring to fall. The flowers are yellow, red, white, or orange depending on the variety grown. Potentillas are easy plants and grow in any well-drained garden soil in sun or partial shade. Remove old and weak branches in spring. Height and spread 1.2 m (4 ft). DISADVANTAGES: none.

Skimmia japonica

A compact evergreen shrub that carries red berries all winter and clusters of white and pink flowers from early spring. It needs a certain amount of shade and prefers slightly acid soil. It is a good shrub for a small town garden. Both male and female plants are needed to produce berries. Height 1.2 m (4 ft). DISADVANTAGES: both male and female plants need to be grown, prefers shade and acid soil.

Viburnum

There is a number of viburnums that should be found in any garden. For the sake of simplicity they can be divided into winter- and spring-flowering varieties.

WINTER FLOWERING
V. x bodnantense

An upright deciduous shrub with fragrant pink or white flowers according to the variety grown, that flowers from late fall to early spring. Height and spread 3 m x 2 m (10 ft x 6 ft).

V. farreri syn. V. fragrans

A similar shrub to *V. x bodnantense* whose leaves turn dark red in the fall. It carries fragrant pink flowers on bare branches from late fall to early spring. It is a very upright shrub and you can cut back new growth after flowering to make it bushier.

V. tinus

(Laurustinus)
Compact, slow-growing, evergreen shrub that has creamy-white, fragrant flowers emerging from pink buds from early winter to the end of spring. It is not a showy plant but has a place in any garden. Height and spread 3 m (10 ft). No pruning required.

SPRING FLOWERING
V. opulus 'Roseum'

(Guelder rose)
A deciduous shrub whose leaves turn red in the fall and carries balls of white flowers in late spring that turn pink as they age. Height and spread 4 m (12 ft).

V. plicatum 'Mariesii'

(Japanese snowball bush)
Another deciduous shrub that has white flowers held on layered branches. It is spectacular when in full flower. Height and spread 3 m x 4 m (10 ft x 13 ft).

31

Opposite: Mahonias have rather spiky leaves that often turn brilliant red and gold in the fall.

Left: *Skimmia japonica* is an excellent shrub for the small garden but male and female plants are needed to produce fruit and flowers.

The soil type within your garden varies with location. If you have acid soil then it will be easy for you to grow a number of the spectacular acid-loving shrubs that only flourish where there is no lime present. The lazy gardener who does not have acid soil in his or her garden is advised not to try and grow these shrubs however much you may like them as garden plants.

32

Opposite: *Rhododendron yakushimanum*. Rhododendrons are the largest genus of plants available for the gardener.

Below: *Camellia japonica* 'Debutante'.

Calluna vulgaris
(Heather, Ling)
The common heather of Scotland makes a good garden plant and is available in a variety of colorsz. It reaches a height of 60 cm (2 ft). Trim after flowering to keep the plants tidy.

Camellia japonica
One of the classic acid-loving plants, camellias need some shade and flower from late winter onwards. The early-flowering varieties need some shelter as their flowers are often browned by late frosts. The flowers are single, semi-double or double in shades of white through to red and are complemented by the neat, glossy evergreen leaves.

Enkianthus campanulatus
An erect deciduous shrub that has clusters of yellow, red-veined flowers and pale green leaves that turn a brilliant yellow, then red in the fall. Height 2.4 m (8 ft).

Erica carnea
(Winter-flowering heather)
Most heathers prefer sun and acid soil but *E. carnea* will tolerate some lime. These are the classic winter-flowering heathers that brighten many a garden in winter. If you are going to grow heathers it is a good idea to devote a whole bed to them as the impact they make is then much greater. They get lost on their own in a mixed border.

Hamamelis mollis
(Witch hazel)
This well-known shrub has curious twisted, yellow or red flowers in winter on bare branches that are very fragrant. The leaves are large and green and turn brilliant colors in the fall. It needs neutral to acid soil to flourish. Height 3 m (10 ft).

Magnolia x soulangeana
There are a very few magnolias that will tolerate chalky soil but the vast majority need neutral to acid soil to flourish. They prefer some shelter from east winds in early spring and their tulip-shaped flowers are one of the finest sights in the early months of the year.

Pieris japonica
Compact evergreen shrubs with clusters of narrow leaves that often emerge bright red in early spring and gradually change to green in the summer, they have spires of white or pink bell-shaped flowers in spring.

Rhododendron
The classic acid-loving shrub available in thousands of varieties that grows best in moist, neutral to acid soil and some shade. Rhododendrons are easy plants given the right conditions. The majority are evergreen but a number of those formerly classified as azaleas are deciduous.

Below: *Weigela* 'Florida Variegata'.

Opposite: The beautiful flowers of the Beauty bush, *Kolkwitzia amabilis.*

Chalk gardens are, traditionally, rather difficult. Choose plants that will tolerate dry thin soil and try to improve the texture of the soil by adding large quantities of garden compost and well-rotted manure.

Corylus avellana 'Contorta'
(Corkscrew hazel)
The twisted or corkscrew hazel is really a small tree that will grow in any reasonable soil in sun or partial shade. It has curious long, yellow catkins in early spring and is always a talking point in the garden. It will reach 3 m (10 ft) but can be pruned to an extent in spring to keep it within bounds.

Deutzia scabra 'Plena'
Deutzias are useful shrubs for small gardens as they do not outgrow their allotted space. *D. s.* 'Plena' is covered with double white flowers in early summer. Some varieties have pink or lilac flowers. They will grow in any well-drained soil in sun or partial shade. Cut back flowering shoots by a third when flowering is over.

Kolkwitzia amabilis
(Beauty bush)
Known as the Beauty bush, this shrub is covered in soft pink flowers in late spring and early summer. The branches hang down as they get older. Prefers full sun and well-drained soil. 3 m x 4 m (10 ft x 13 ft).

Lavatera 'Barnsley'
(Tree mallow)
The tree mallow is a very popular, semi-evergreen, shrub that must have well-drained soil and full sun to show its best. It has a mass of pale pink flowers with darker centers from summer until the late fall. They are very vigorous and should be cut back hard each year in early spring. 2 m x 2 m (6 ft x 6 ft).

Symphoricarpos x doorenbosii 'Mother of Pearl'
(Snowberry)
The common snowberry has small pink flowers in summer followed by white berries that often remain on the bushes all winter. Birds don't like them. 'Mother of Pearl' has lovely pinkish, white berries and *S. orbiculatus* has red berries. The plants can make a good informal hedge and will grow almost anywhere. 1.5 m x 1.5 m (5 ft x 5 ft).

Weigela florida 'Foliis Purpureis'
Weigelas will grow in almost any well-drained soil and while they prefer sun they will also tolerate some shade. They have funnel-shaped pink, red and white flowers. 'Foliis Purpureis' has bronze-green foliage. It is a good idea to cut back the flowering stems by one third after flowering, otherwise the plants become rather straggly. 1 m x 1.5 m (3 ft x 5 ft).

35

Above: *Crataegus laevigata* **'Paul's Scarlet' is one of the most popular hawthorns in the garden.**

Right: *Cotinus coggygria* **grown for its red and orange fall leaves.**

Opposite: *Acer palmatum* **'Dissectum Ornatum' has leaves with white markings. All maples have brilliant fall color.**

Fall is an important time in the garden and even the lazy gardener should try and grow some trees or shrubs specially for their fall color. There is a large number to choose from.

Acer

(Maple)

Maple trees are famous for their fall color. There is a large number available and they do best in well-drained, neutral to slightly acid soil, some varieties may need some protection in hard winters. *A. rubrum* 'October Glory' has particularly brilliant red leaves in the fall, while the dwarf varieties of *A. palmatum*, the Japanese maple, are suitable for small gardens.

Cotinus coggygria

(Smoke bush)

A shrub grown for its fall color when the light green leaves turn yellow then orange, then red. It has light, feathery, fawn-colored flowers held aloft on stalks. It grows in any reasonably well-drained garden soil and prefers full sun. Pruning is not really necessary. 2.5 m x 2.5 m (8 ft x 8 ft).

Crataegus crus-galli

(Cockspur thorn)

The cockspur thorn is a small tree that bears a mass of white flowers in spring followed by multitudes of red berries in the fall. The leaves are glossy green and turn gradually to a brilliant scarlet. Height 4.5 m (15 ft).

Liriodendron tulipifera

(Tulip tree)

Not a tree for the normal garden as it can grow as high as 30 m (100 ft), the tulip tree is nevertheless a spectacular sight in the fall when the square leaves turn a brilliant yellow. It also has large greenish-white, magnolia-like flowers splashed with orange, in midsummer. They prefer slightly acid soil.

Rhus typhina

(Stag's horn sumach)

The stag's horn sumach is a large spreading shrub and is not suitable for small gardens. It has furry brown young shoots in spring and dark green leaves that turn vivid orange and red in the fall. The flower spikes last through the winter and are held up on the ends of the branches. 4.5 m x 6 m (15 ft x 20 ft).

Stephanandra tanakae

A medium-sized suckering shrub that has clusters of small white and yellow elder-like flowers in summer and leaves that turn golden yellow and orange in the fall. Prefers sun and moist well-drained soil. 2 m (7 ft).

12 GOOD CONIFERS

There are really rather a lot of conifers; some, even, are deciduous and drop their needles, and some have leaves, not needles, but for common everyday purposes most are evergreen, most have needles, and the range of sizes and colors available is enormous. Conifers are the last word in instant gardening and they give form and shape to any garden, however new. A word of warning: it is a mistake to try to plant large trees. They resent being moved and it is much better to buy small container-grown trees from a specialist nursery.

39

Left: *Picea pungens* 'Koster',
a variety of the Colorado
spruce, is grown for its blue-
grey foliage. It can reach a
height of 15 m (50 ft).

Below: *Taxus baccata* **forms a dense hedge that can be clipped to shape. The clippings are used in the treatment of cancer.**

Opposite: *Chamaecyparis lawsoniana.* **The species tree can reach a height of 40 m (130 ft).**

THERE IS A NUMBER OF DIFFERENT TYPES

Abies koreana
(Korean fir)
The Korean fir is a striking tree grown for its violet-purple cones and dark green and silver needles. It can be grown in any good garden soil. Reaches 3 m (10 ft).

Cedrus atlantica 'Glauca'
(Atlantic cedar)
The blue Atlantic cedar, widely grown as a specimen tree, is best suited to large gardens. It eventually makes a very large tree but usually reaches about 3 m (10 ft) after ten years or so. It has silver-blue needles and can be pruned into a columnar shape if space is limited.

Chamaecyparis lawsoniana 'Ellwood's Gold'
(False cypress)
A slow-growing false cypress with golden tips at the end of the branches. It is a popular tree and often found in small gardens. Height 1.2 m (4 ft) after 8-10 years.

x Cupressocyparis leylandii 'Castlewellan'
(Leyland cypress)
If you have a pinetum you might consider growing one Leyland cypress, x *Cupressocyparis leylandii*, as a specimen tree. The mature, dark green tree makes the most imposing column over 30 m (100 ft) high. Alas they are usually grown as a hedge and, with few exceptions, they are the cause of more trouble than any other single garden plant. They also need to be trimmed at least three times a year to keep them within bounds. If you feel that you have to plant a hedge of leylandii, choose the variety 'Castlewellan', it is slower growing and has attractive golden foliage.

Cupressus arizonica var. glabra
(Arizona cypress)
The smooth Arizona cypress has good, blue-grey foliage, reddish-purple bark and is fully hardy, a number of the traditional cypresses found in the Mediterranean are less so. It is slow growing and reaches a height of 4 m (13 ft) after 8-10 years, a fully mature tree may grow to 15 m (50 ft).

Juniperus squamata 'Blue Star'
(Flaky juniper)
A low spreading juniper with quite startling light blue-green foliage in winter that turns to creamy yellow in spring and then gradually darkens to blue-green as summer proceeds. Very suitable for a rockery or a heather border. Height and spread 40 cm x 1 m (16 in x 3 ft).

Picea pungens 'Koster'
(Colorado spruce)
Spruces may be difficult to establish when young but once they have got going they will

tolerate poor conditions.
P. p. 'Koster', a variety of the
Colorado spruce, is one of the
most popular of the blue spruces.
Height of a mature tree 12 m (40
ft) or more but it will take many
years to grow this large and reaches
2 m (6.5 ft) after 8-10 years.

Pinus mugo 'Gnom'

(Dwarf mountain pine)
A variety of the dwarf mountain
pine, this is a good rounded shrub
for the rockery. It grows very
slowly indeed and reaches 60 cm
(2 ft) in 10 years.

Taxus baccata

(Yew)
One of the very best hedging
plants, the common yew does not
grow as slowly as is commonly
believed. If a yew hedge is planted
in prepared ground and fed each
year with good mulch and
compost then you can expect a
growth rate of 25 cm (1 ft) a year,
possibly slightly more. A mature
yew hedge forms a dense
evergreen barrier. They need
clipping twice a year in summer
and the fall. An old yew hedge will
stand drastic renovation.

Thuja plicata

(Western red cedar)
A rival to the yew as a hedging
plant the western red cedar is
quicker growing, but the final
hedge is less dense. It is far more
easily controlled than leylandii.

Clip twice a year in spring and fall.
Both yew and cedar may be grown
as specimen trees in a large
garden.

Tsuga canadensis 'Pendula'

(Eastern hemlock)
Mature specimens of *T. canadensis*,
the eastern hemlock, can reach 25
m (80 ft), and *T. heterophylla*, the
western hemlock, may grow as
high as 40 m (130 ft). There are
smaller varieties available for the
gardener. *T. c.* 'Pendula' is a lovely
weeping conifer and forms a
mound of spreading, hanging
branches. It will eventually reach 4
m (13 ft) but it has a slow rate of
growth and will take a long time
to achieve that size.

Below: Holly can be planted as a hedge but it takes some time to reach a good height. Some varieties, such as *Ilex aquifolium* 'Silver Queen', have white or creamy margins to their leaves.

Opposite top: *Rosa rugosa* can be clipped to make an informal hedge.

Opposite bottom: A beech hedge is one of the most popular of all. They grow best in fairly light soils.

The most commonly used plants for hedging are privet, and the evergreen conifers, yew and western red cedar. Box is the favorite plant for a small formal hedge, but both box and privet require trimming two or three times a year and are not recommended for the lazy gardener. Hawthorn (crataegus) is often used as a deciduous hedge as is *Berberis thunbergii* – both have the advantage of being particularly prickly and invader-proof. Other hedging plants include escallonia, elaeagnus, winter honeysuckle (*Lonicera nitida*), *Cotoneaster monogyna* and pyracantha; small flowering hedging plants include fuchsia, lavender and potentilla.

Of the hedging plants described below some are common, some not so common.

Abelia x grandiflora

If you live in a particularly sheltered part of the country then you might consider planting an unusual hedge of abelia, a plant commonly used for hedging on the continent. Abelias are evergreen or semi-evergreen shrubs with pink-tinged white flowers from midsummer right through the fall but they are not fully hardy and need protection if grown in colder areas. They grow in any well-drained soil and will reach 3 m x 3.5 m (10 ft x 12 ft) in a favorable position. Grown as a shrub they require minimal pruning. Trim in early spring if used as a hedging plant.

Carpinus betulus

(Hornbeam)
Hornbeam has many of the properties of beech and makes an excellent hedge. It is a better plant to use where the soil is a bit wet and heavy. The leaves stay on the hedge all winter and only drop when the new buds start into growth the following spring. Trim once a year in late summer.

Fagus sylvatica

(Beech)
Possibly the favorite deciduous hedging plant, beech hedges make dense screens throughout the year as they retain the old golden leaves on

the plants all winter. The old leaves are then replaced by new pale green leaves in spring. Beech hedges planted with one of the copper-leaved varieties every four of five plants can be particularly attractive. Trim in late summer.

Ilex aquifolium

(Holly)

Common holly makes a dense, prickly hedge, evergreen with good dark or variegated leaves, according to the variety planted. It is however rather slow growing and planting a holly hedge can be considered an investment in the future. Trim in late summer.

Prunus laurocerasus and P. lusitanica

(Common laurel and Portuguese laurel)

Common laurel and Portuguese laurel both make good, dense, evergreen hedges with their large pointed leaves. Prune in late summer. They may require cutting back quite severely.

Rosa rugosa

(Rose)

Some roses make the most attractive informal hedge but the accent is on informal as they will not stand regular clipping and shaping. The best are the rugosa roses and the most commonly used varieties are 'Roseraie de l'Haÿ', large purple flowers and good green foliage and 'Blanche Double de Coubert'.

6 SMALL SHRUBS

If you garden in a town you need to be very careful about the shrubs that you plant. Many shrubs, even the smallest, eventually outgrow their allotted space and nothing is worse than having to dig up a lovely plant simply because it has become too large and unmanageable. If you plan carefully and check before you buy then this may be avoided.

Brachyglottis Dunedin Group 'Sunshine'

This plant used to be called *Senecio* 'Sunshine' and you may well still find it under that name in nurseries. It is a good plant for a grey and silver garden with silvery-grey leaves in spring that turn grey-green as summer wears on. It likes a sunny, dry position in the garden. It has yellow daisy-like flowers in summer and the plant should be trimmed back after flowering to prevent it becoming straggly. Height 1 m (3 ft).

Cistus x cyprius

(Rock rose)

Do not attempt to grow rock roses if you have heavy soil, a cold frosty garden, or can only offer a shaded position. Apart from these disadvantages they are charming small shrubs with white, pink and red flowers that flower for two months from early summer, each flower lasting for one day only. They thrive in the other problem gardening positions, light chalky soil, sandy and seaside gardens and dry sunny borders. Replace any winter casualties with pot-grown specimens in spring.

Fuchsia magellanica

There are so many varieties of fuchsia with their bell-shaped white, pink and red flowers that the choice is difficult. Many, however, are frost tender and must be overwintered in a greenhouse if they are to survive to next spring. The varieties of *F. magellanica*, the hardy fuchsia, are the most common and the plants can be grown as a flowering hedge in the milder parts of the country. Otherwise, if the plant is damaged by frost, cut the shoots down to just above ground level in spring. Hardy fuchsias are vigorous plants and this treatment keeps them within bounds.

Lavandula

(Lavender)

Lavender is a favorite small shrub, in medieval times grown in fields for its scented flowers. It makes a good low hedge and is frequently found used as an edging plant for a rose walk. *L. angustifolia* 'Hidcote' has deep purple flowers and silver leaves, *L. x intermedia*, old English lavender, has grey-green leaves and light blue to purple flowers. Trim off the flower stalks when flowering is over and trim back the bushes to shape in spring, they can be cut back quite hard.

TIPS
FOR THE lazy GARDENER

Hypericum calcynum

(Rose of Sharon, St John's wort)
Hypericum is really a spreading
subshrub that will reach a height of
45 cm (18 in). It has brilliant
yellow flowers from midsummer
onwards. It is usually grown as a
ground-cover plant and is most
useful for covering rough banks.
Cut back hard every other year in
early spring to keep it in shape.

Santolina chamaecyparissus

(Cotton lavender)
Known as cotton lavender, this small
shrub will grow as high as 60 cm (2
ft). It is grown for its silvery-grey,
aromatic foliage. It has small yellow
flowers in summer but some
gardeners cut them off as they are not
particularly attractive. It can be grown
as a small hedge and needs full sun
and well-drained soil to thrive.

45

Opposite top: *Fuchsia
magellanica* **is the hardiest
fuchsia and requires severe
pruning to keep it within
bounds.**

**Opposite bottom: The
silvery-grey leaves of the
Brachyglottis Dunedin Group
'Sunshine'.**

Left: *Lavandula stoechas*,
**French lavender, has a rather
thistle-like flowerhead. It is
very fragrant.**

Many gardeners inherit trees from gardeners who have gone before them. If you have a small garden then there will usually only be room for one, at the most two, small trees and these have to be chosen carefully so that they do not dominate the site. The problem in small town gardens is more often cutting back existing, inappropriate trees planted a number of years ago. Such trees may well be subject to tree preservation orders and permission will be needed to cut them down, however badly this needs doing. If you have a new garden then you can plant a tree and this needs to be chosen carefully. Choose a tree that will not grow too large for the site too quickly, and choose a tree that grows well in the soil you can offer it. There is a wide choice.

Betula pendula
(Silver birch)
The silver birch so loved by many gardeners will eventually reach a height of 10-13 m (30-40 ft). However it takes some time to grow that big and its graceful habit with its thin, hanging branches and silver, white peeling bark gives it the appearance of being a smaller tree than it is. It grows in any reasonable soil in sun or partial shade. They are shallow rooted and newly planted trees may need watering in dry spells.

Crataegus laevigata 'Paul's Scarlet'
(Hawthorn)
The hawthorn or 'may' is a much underrated tree with clusters of white flowers in spring, followed by vivid scarlet berries in the fall. The leaves turn a golden yellow in the fall. The variety 'Paul's Scarlet' is commonly grown in gardens and makes a good specimen when grown in a lawn. It has double red flowers with small white centers. Height 4.5 m (15 ft).

Laburnum x watereri 'Vossii'
This is the best variety of laburnum. It has a fairly upright growth habit and has exceptionally long tresses (racemes) of bright yellow flowers in early summer. It will reach a height of 7.5 m (25 ft) but takes some time to do so. Laburnums do not have a very robust rooting system and may benefit from staking. They will grow in any but waterlogged soil and can be grown in full sun or partial shade. Beware, beware, the whole plant is poisonous, the black seeds that follow the flowers in the fall, particularly so. Do not plant in a garden where there are small children.

Malus 'John Downie'
(Crab apple)
Any apple or pear tree would be a good choice for a small garden.

They are both grafted on to various rootstocks that govern their rate of growth and small varieties are available. Check the size with the nursery if you are tempted. They have lovely blossom and produce fruit to eat. Fruit trees, however, absolutely must be pruned if they are to flourish and bear apples or pears. This is not in the province of the lazy gardener so an alternative choice is one of the ornamental crabs that only requires spindly and straggly shoots to be removed in winter, even that is not necessary. 'John Downie' is an excellent variety with largish red fruit, 'Golden Hornet' has bright yellow fruit.

Prunus
(Flowering cherry)
Ornamental cherries are spectacular trees, familiar to everyone, with massed ranks of white or pink blossom in spring that emerges before the leaves. Many have colorful bark as an added bonus. They come in all shapes and sizes, from slender and upright to broad and weeping. If you want to plant one choose carefully and ask for professional help. There are suitable cherries for most gardens so don't just pick one up in the local garden center as it may grow far too big for the position you can offer it. They grow in any well-drained garden soil and like some lime.

Sorbus aucuparia
(Mountain ash)
The mountain ash is a common tree in gardens and in the wild. It is a good tree for a small garden with excellent fall color. It has white flowers in spring, large clusters of red fruit in the fall and green leaves that turn yellow, and then red. There is a number of other species and varieties that have white, yellow and orange berries but the gardener usually has little time to admire them as they are much favored by the birds. 8 m (25 ft).

Opposite: The yellow flowers of the laburnum make a charming picture in early summer.

Below: *Prunus* 'Taihaku', the great white cherry, showing all its glory in spring. There are suitable cherry trees for all gardens.

47

Clematis

Clematis are lovely colorful climbers for walls and scrambling through trees and shrubs.

C. montana will also quickly cover a fence or railings. The most complicated question about clematis is how they should be pruned. There are three groups and in an ideal world each needs to be treated differently. This can be a problem for most (lazy) gardeners as recognition of the plants in different groups is difficult without a really good color recognition guide.

Some simple advice:

1 If the clematis flowers for the first time between winter and summer then only prune if it is getting too large for its allotted space or too untidy. This may well be the case as some early-flowering varieties such as *C. montana* are very vigorous. Cut them back after flowering to fit the space available.

2 If the clematis flowers for the first time in summer don't prune it until you have to. Then the simplest thing to do is to cut the plant down to 60 cm (2 ft) from the ground early in the spring. You will have fewer flowers in that year but the plant will be tidier.

3 If the plant flowers for the first time from summer onwards, cut it down to 60 cm (2 ft) above the ground early in spring every year. Cut just above a strong pair of buds.

Favorite clematis include:
C. montana, spring-flowering, white, *C.* 'Jackmanii Superba', large purple flowers, summer onwards, 'Comtesse de Bouchaud' large, pink, flowers, summer onwards, 'Henryi', large creamy white, summer onwards, *C. alpina* 'Frances Rivis', blue bell-shaped flowers, spring-summer.

Clematis are adaptable plants and there are varieties that will grow in most garden positions including north-facing walls.

Consult a specialist nursery for advice. All clematis like to have their feet cold, most gardeners position a paving slab over the roots after planting; they appreciate a mulch in early spring and grow best in fertile well-drained soil.

If you are planting a clematis to grow up a wall dig the planting hole at least 30 cm (18 in) away from the wall and train the plant towards the wall by tying it in to a cane or wire trellis. Finally all clematis must be planted deeply. Plant so that the soil level is above the first buds. This helps to prevent clematis wilt.

Hedera

Ivy is not everyone's idea of their favorite garden plant but it can be very useful. It is evergreen, covers a wall quickly and grows anywhere. If you want to cover a north wall then you should choose one of the green varieties available. If you can offer some sun then one of the many variegated ivies is more colorful. Ivies also grow at different rates so measure your wall and check with your nursery before buying. They will need some cutting back to keep them in check and should not be allowed to grow into roofs or gutters.

Favorite varieties include: *H. canariensis* 'Gloire de Marengo', large light green silvery leaves, variegated creamy white (only grow Canary island ivies if you can offer

Opposite top: Ivy (*Hedera helix* 'White Knight').

Opposite bottom: *Clematis montana*.

Top: *Clematis* 'Fuji-musume'.

Right: Ivy makes an excellent wall covering.

them some shelter, they are not fully hardy); *H. colchica* 'Dentata', very large darkish green leaves; *H. colchica* 'Sulphur Heart', better known as 'Paddy's Pride', mid-green leaves with a pronounced yellow tinge; *H. helix* (Common ivy or English ivy), dark green, three- or five-lobed leaves. *H. helix* varieties include: 'Anne Marie', green leaves with creamy-white margins; 'Glacier', grey-green leaves with white margins and 'Goldheart', green leaves splashed with golden yellow in the center.

Hydrangea petiolaris

The climbing hydrangea is a vigorous plant that will cover a large area and prefers shade to sun. It is deciduous. It may take a year or two to get going and will require some support during this time but after a while it is a magnificent sight, covered with white lacecap flowers from summer onwards. Pruning is not necessary but the plant will require cutting back to keep it within bounds in the course of time.

Lonicera periclymenum

(English honeysuckle)
The lovely English honeysuckle, found in many gardens, is wonderfully scented, the garden varieties 'Belgica', white flowers that turn yellow, blooms in early summer, and 'Serotina', white flowers marked with purple on the outside, blooms from summer to fall. Honeysuckles grow quickly and will reach 7 m (23 ft) in a few years. Honeysuckles have one disadvantage. They are untidy plants and are best grown where they can scramble unheeded through an old tree. If they are grown against a wall they are best pruned fairly hard to keep them reasonably tidy. Do this as soon as flowering is over as they flower on the laterals produced from the previous year's growth.

Parthenocissus

(Boston ivy, Virginia creeper)
Well-known climbers that make amazing fall color clinging to the sides of houses. Their brilliant display of fall color lasts but a short time, three to four weeks at the most, and then the leaves drop with the first frosts of the fall. Much the best varieties are *P. tricuspidata* (Boston ivy), *P. quinquefolia* (Virginia creeper) and *P. henryana* with its variegated leaves. All these have green leaves before their moment of fall glory. Parthenocissus likes well-drained soil but will grow in sun or shade. *P. henryana* is most colorful when grown on a north or east-facing wall. Cut the plant back each year when the leaves have fallen to prevent it reaching into the roof and gutters of the house where it will damage the tiles and block the drains. Pull the old tendrils away from the wall. They come away quite easily with relatively little effort.

Pyracantha
(Firethorn)

Pyracantha, firethorn, is the classic evergreen wall shrub, with dark green leaves. It has clusters of white flowers in late spring followed by red berries in the fall and is often trained formally against a frame. It will flourish on a north wall and needs training so that it forms a basic shape. This is easy to do as the plant is most adaptable and can be grown around doors and windows. After it has been trained and the main framework formed, it will need cutting back in midsummer every year, removing all growth pointing away from the wall to within 7.5-10 cm (3-4 in) of the main framework and any branches that are too congested. This is not the most pleasant gardening job as the plant has vicious spikes. Ideally the plant should be trimmed again in early fall to reveal the berries, but the lazy gardener will not bother with this.

Opposite: *Parthenocissus henryana*, the Chinese Virginia creeper, has white-veined leaves that turn brilliant red in the fall.

Below: *Lonicera periclymenum* 'Belgica', Early Dutch honeysuckle, has white flowers streaked with red on the outside. The flowers turn yellow as they mature.

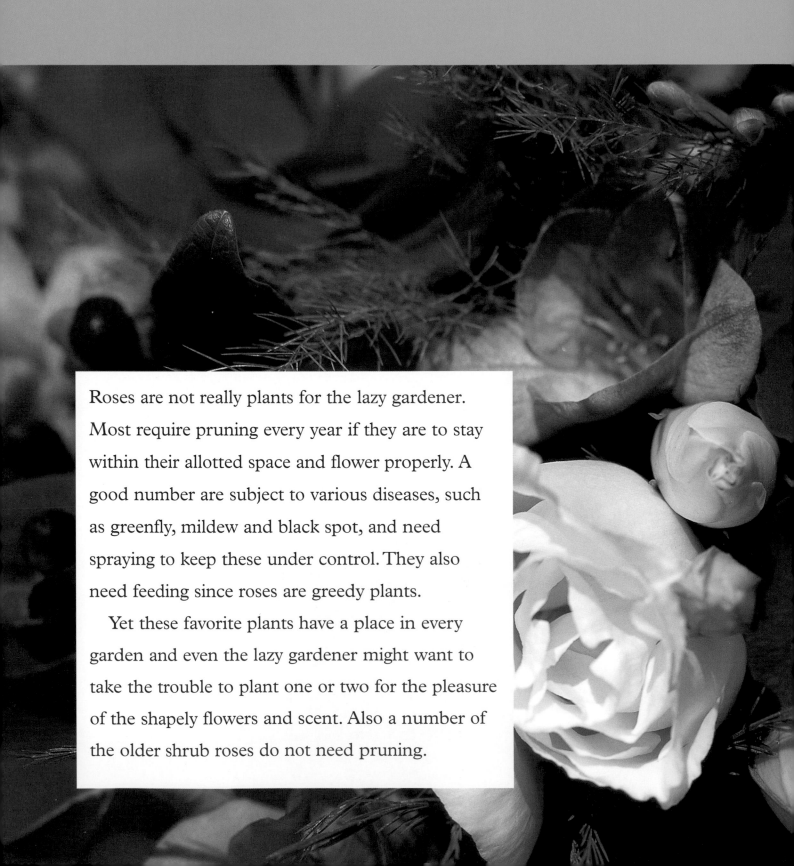

ROSES

Roses are not really plants for the lazy gardener. Most require pruning every year if they are to stay within their allotted space and flower properly. A good number are subject to various diseases, such as greenfly, mildew and black spot, and need spraying to keep these under control. They also need feeding since roses are greedy plants.

Yet these favorite plants have a place in every garden and even the lazy gardener might want to take the trouble to plant one or two for the pleasure of the shapely flowers and scent. Also a number of the older shrub roses do not need pruning.

TIPS
FOR THE lazy GARDENER

53

Left: Roses are probably the best-loved flowers in the garden but they do require attention from the gardener. The reward is a wonderful display of scented blooms.

ROSES

DONT'S

Consider growing rambler roses unless you have a large garden with old apple or fruit trees that you no longer care much about, or a house with high walls and a high ladder that you are prepared to climb, erect a framework of wire, and then prune and tie in the rose each year.

Consider planting a dedicated rose bed, unless you have a large garden and want to devote one part of it to roses.

Try and grow roses in a shady position without checking carefully on the requirements of the type you want to plant. Most roses need at least 3-4 hours sunshine a day to flower well, although there are some tough old varieties and modern hybrids that will grow in shade. Some of these are listed below.

Choose large roses if you have a very small garden, many roses, even the ordinary hybrid tea and floribunda roses, can grown fairly large, fairly quickly.

Plant new roses where old roses have recently been grown. Soil becomes rose sick. If you have to do this, you need to excavate a large hole, remove several barrowloads of soil, line the hole with cardboard and replace the soil with new and then plant the rose in this. This usually works but is not absolutely guaranteed.

Plant old-fashioned shrub roses unless you have enough room in the garden. Most of them grow fairly large.

Plant old-fashioned roses if you want repeat flowers throughout the summer and fall, most only flower once.

DO'S

Choose your rose with care. Check the size, vigor, color and disease resistance before you buy. Be particularly careful about color, you can achieve some ghastly color clashes with some of the brightly colored modern varieties.

Buy bare-root roses from a reputable nursery and plant them in the fall. They will make better plants than container-grown roses.

Check on the requirements of the roses you buy, and try to give them the conditions they prefer.

THREE SUGGESTIONS

55

No one gardener has the right to dictate to another, especially a lazy one, but if you have a small garden and want to grow some roses here are three suggestions.

If you have a mixed border, plant two or three roses towards the back and then they will add color and focus throughout the summer. Choose repeat-flowering hybrid teas or floribundas. A number of hybrid tea roses (roses that carry a single flower on a stalk) have large, rather overblown, flowers and need space to display their charms at their best. Floribundas (roses that have a cluster of flowers usually smaller than hybrid teas) might be better.

If you have a shrubbery with enough room then add two or three old-fashioned shrub roses, or plant a group of three modern English roses.

Modern climbers. There is a number of modern climbers that are relatively slow-growing and are ideal for growing up walls and trellises particularly in small town gardens.

Left: *R.* **Mountbatten.**

Above: *R* **'Louise Odier'.**

All these roses can be planted in small borders. Bright red colors in a border make a statement and attract attention, white helps to link one color with another, and pale yellow and pink will usually blend perfectly with the flowers of other plants. Prune all of them by cutting them in half, (horizontally) early in spring. Mulch well, spray if you see signs of disease.

56

Above: *R* Peace. A perennially popular hybrid-tea rose introduced in 1945.

'Apricot Nectar' (floribunda).
Apricot-yellow in color with small sprays of large flowers, rather like a hybrid tea. Fragrant. Quite vigorous and will reach 1 m (3 ft).

Chicago Peace (hybrid tea).
A sport of the famous Peace rose with much pinker flowers that shade to yellow at the base. Very slightly fragrant. 1.2 m (4 ft).

Elina (hybrid tea).
Pale primrose-yellow with flowers that are not too large. 1 m (3 ft).

Evelyn Fison (floribunda).
A well-known, strong, scarlet rose with dark green leaves, disease resistant. 1 m (3 ft).

Margaret Merril (floribunda).
A lovely rose with white flowers that open from slightly pink buds. Exceptionally fragrant. 80 cm (2.5 ft).

Velvet Fragrance (hybrid tea).
Dark red, a strong rose that blooms prolifically throughout the summer. Strong fragrance. 1.5 m (4½ ft).

pink
red
yellow white

Right: Climbing roses in complementary colors interspersed with honeysuckle frame a herbaceous border dominated by erigeron, fuchsias and valerian.

6 SMALLER CLIMBING ROSES

If you have the space and want to grow large climbing roses there are many available. Below is a selection of roses that will not grow at a rate of knots and can be contained within most modern gardens.

Breath of Life (modern climber)
Pinkish-apricot hybrid tea-shaped, large flowers, fragrant. 2.4 m (8 ft). Little pruning necessary: cut out dead wood and shorten side shoots by a half where possible.

'Compassion' (modern climber)
Fairly large salmon pink flowers, tinted with orange. Very fragrant. Strong bushy growth that may need to be controlled. 3 m (10 ft). Prune by cutting out dead wood.

'Climbing Iceberg' (floribunda)
The climbing form of the favorite floribunda with graceful white flowers. No fragrance. It will require tying in but needs little pruning. 3 m (10 ft).

'Climbing Lady Sylvia' (hybrid tea)
A sport of the famous hybrid tea, Ophelia, with slightly deeper pink coloring and the rich fragrance of the parent. Perfect buds. 3.5 m (12 ft). Cut out dead wood and shorten side shoots by two-thirds in spring.

Golden Showers (modern climber)
A very popular rose that flowers continuously throughout the summer. It carries large semi-double, golden-yellow flowers that fade as they age. The flowers have a good fragrance. It is one of the best roses for a north wall. 3 m (10 ft).

'White Cockade' (modern climber)
A slow-growing, beautiful, pure white rose with some fragrance. Perfect hybrid tea-shaped buds. An ideal climbing rose for a trellis in a small town garden. 2 m (7 ft). Cut out dead wood and shorten side shoots by two-thirds in spring.

Opposite: *R.* **'Climbing Iceberg'.**

Opposite: *R. xanthina* 'Canary Bird' is a popular variety of the species rose with an arching habit that can be grown as a shrub or trained against a wall. It carries single, deep yellow flowers and has a lovely musk-like fragrance. It is not always totally reliable and for preference should be given the protection of a south or south-west wall.

No rose will grow in complete shade, overshadowed by trees, or in woodland. Nevertheless there is a number that will do quite well in poor soil conditions, several climbers that will survive on a north wall, and many that tolerate partial shade perfectly happily. The chief class of rose that tolerates poor conditions is the old-fashioned alba roses. The flowers are really either pink or white but they are disease-free, require no pruning apart from cutting out dead wood and are superbly fragrant. Unfortunately they only flower once a year.

'Félicité Parmentier' (alba)
Beautiful, large, pale pink, multi-petalled flowers of old rose shape. Not very fragrant but grows into a relatively short and bushy plant. 1.2 x 1.2 m (4 ft x 4 ft).

'Mme Legras de St Germain' (alba)
A lovely rose with perfect pompon-like flowers that open flat and then form a ball. The flowers are white with a faint tinge of yellow. Very fragrant. 1.5 m x 1.2 m (5 ft x 4 ft).

'Maigold' (modern climber)
Bronze-yellow, semi-double flowers with good glossy foliage. Vigorous and prickly it survives happily on a north wall but really only flowers once. Very fragrant. 3.5 m (12 ft).

'New Dawn' (modern climber)
A popular rose for many years, 'New Dawn' has masses of pale silvery pink flowers that repeat throughout the summer, and shiny mid-green leaves. It is hardy, vigorous, will grow on a north wall and is very fragrant. 3 m (10 ft).

R. pimpinellifolia 'Dunwich Rose'
(The Scottish rose, Burnet rose). *R. pimpinellifolia*, the Burnet rose and its varieties, flowers early in the year at the end of spring and early summer. As a group they form a low-growing shrub and carry a mass of single, white or yellow flowers on arching branches. The Dunwich rose is one of the best varieties with pale lemon-yellow flowers. They are excellent roses for poor sandy soil and do not require any pruning.

'Queen of Denmark' (alba)
Sometimes called 'Königen von Dänemarck' this is one of the best alba roses with large, quartered, pink flowers and lovely grey-green foliage. Very strong fragrance. 1.5 m x 1.2 m (5 ft x 4 ft).

6 SHRUB ROSES

Opposite: *R.* 'Ballerina' is a modern shrub rose that carries a mass of single flowers on multiple heads in pink and white. It is extremely reliable and not too large, flowering continuously throughout the summer. It has little or no scent.

There are various groups of shrub roses and people toss the names around so lightly that it is very easy to become confused. The older varieties such as; gallicas, albas, damasks, centifolias (The Rose of Provence), moss, china, Portland, Bourbon, and hybrid perpetuals have different properties and characteristics and some even repeat-flower.

More modern shrub roses include rugosas and hybrid musks, and there are also the wild (species) roses and their varieties found in many gardens. A shrub rose is exactly what it says it is – a shrub that is a rose – when planning a garden this is the thing to bear in mind. None of them really need pruning, indeed some resent it bitterly and may well turn their toes up if pruned harshly.

'Ballerina' (shrub)
A fairly modern polyantha shrub rose that carries a profusion of pale pink, single flowers with white centers. They are much the same color as apple blossom. It is most reliable, flowers all summer and has a slight scent.

'Belle de Crécy' (gallica)
The flowers of this rose open a rich pink and then turn to soft violet, the foliage is grey green. Very fragrant. 1.2 m x 1 m (4 ft x 3 ft).

'Buff Beauty' (hybrid musk)
Warm apricot-yellow flowers held in large clusters. The flowers themselves are large and rather crumpled. Repeat flowering. Good fragrance with dark green leaves. May need spraying against mildew. 1.5 x 1.5 m (5 ft x 5 ft).

'Chapeau de Napoléon' (centifolia)
This may be found listed as *R. x centifolia* 'Cristata'. It has pure pink, large flowers with typical old rose cabbage-like character, centifolias make open shrubs and the branches often droop with the weight of the flowers. Very fragrant. 1.2 x 1.2 m (4 ft x 4 ft).

'Nevada' (modern shrub)
A wonderful sight when in flower in early summer when the whole bush is smothered by large, creamy-white, semi-double flowers. It flowers again intermittently throughout the summer but the first flush is outstanding. Slight fragrance. It has an arching habit and will eventually make a large shrub 2 m x 2 m (7 ft x 7 ft).

'Zigeunerknabe' (Bourbon)
Also called Gipsy Boy this rose dates from 1909. It has rather small, violet-purple flowers with pronounced yellow stamens. It is hardy, prickly, disease-resistant and fragrant, the stems may need some support. It will reach 1.5 m x 1.2 m (5 ft x 4 ft).

6 MODERN ENGLISH ROSES

Opposite: R. Graham Thomas, a modern English rose named after one of the famous gardeners of the 20th century who resurrected many old roses.

Modern English roses are one of the triumphs of modern gardening. They were bred by David Austin and combine the lush flowers of old-fashioned roses, the fragrance typical of those roses, and the ability to repeat-flower throughout the season. David Austin recommends that they are planted in groups of two or three of the same variety and they will then grow together to form a dense shrub that makes a definite statement in the garden. There are many to choose from, some more vigorous than others. The selection below lists one of each of the main colors available. Prune them by shortening the shoots by one third to a half each year. Remove old growth when the bushes become congested.

Ambridge Rose
Deep apricot pink flowers that get paler at the edges. Has a neat bushy growth. 75 cm (2.5 ft)

Cottage Rose
Bears a succession of medium-sized, cupped, warm pink flowers throughout the summer with a delicate old rose fragrance. Geoff Hamilton is another lovely pink rose. 1 m x 75 cm (3.5 ft x 2.5 ft).

Heritage
Pale soft blush pink flowers that are not too large with an outstanding fragrance. The growth is lax at first but it builds up into a good bushy shrub. 1.2 m x 1.2 m (4 ft x 4 ft).

Graham Thomas
Named after one of the great rose gardeners of the twentieth century, this rose has clear yellow flowers and an upright and vigorous growth. It is very fragrant. 1.2 m x 1.2 m (4 ft x 4 ft).

L.D. Braithwaite
A number of English roses have flowers with outstanding deep red, purple and mauve coloring. This rose has deep red flowers that are almost perfect in their form. Fragrant. 1 m x 1 m (3 ft x 3 ft) or larger.

Winchester Cathedral
A lovely white rose that continues to carry large crumpled white flowers all summer. Fragrant. 1.2 m x 1.2 m (4 ft x 4 ft).

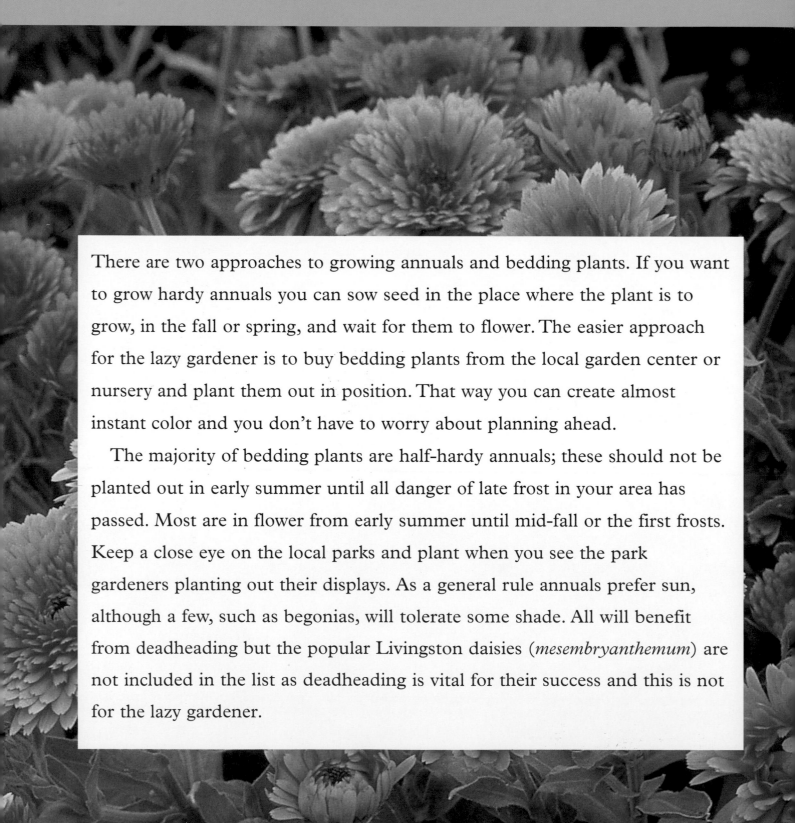

There are two approaches to growing annuals and bedding plants. If you want to grow hardy annuals you can sow seed in the place where the plant is to grow, in the fall or spring, and wait for them to flower. The easier approach for the lazy gardener is to buy bedding plants from the local garden center or nursery and plant them out in position. That way you can create almost instant color and you don't have to worry about planning ahead.

The majority of bedding plants are half-hardy annuals; these should not be planted out in early summer until all danger of late frost in your area has passed. Most are in flower from early summer until mid-fall or the first frosts. Keep a close eye on the local parks and plant when you see the park gardeners planting out their displays. As a general rule annuals prefer sun, although a few, such as begonias, will tolerate some shade. All will benefit from deadheading but the popular Livingston daisies (*mesembryanthemum*) are not included in the list as deadheading is vital for their success and this is not for the lazy gardener.

NG PLANTS

67

**Left: Marigolds are one of the
most popular annuals for
flower and vegetable garden.**

Above: *Ageratum houstonianum* 'Blue Danube'.

Ageratum

(Floss flower)
Most varieties available are blue, although pink and white varieties can be found. They have masses of powder-puff type flowers and are excellent plants for edging a border. Some taller varieties are available. Height and spread 15-23 cm (6-9 in).

Begonia semperflorens

Small fibrous-rooted begonias make good bedding plants and will flower from early summer right through until the fall. They are usually white, pink or red and some have bronze foliage. Height 10-30 cm (4-12 in). Spread 15-20 cm (6-8 in).

Cineraria maritima

Grown as a foliage plant the silver-grey leaves contrast with the bright flowers of summer bedding. It does have insignificant yellow flowers. Height 20-30 cm (8-12 in). Spread 23-30 cm (9-12 in).

Dianthus chinensis

(Annual carnation)
There is a number of varieties available in contrasting colors. They have fringed petals and do not need staking. Sweet smelling flowers throughout summer. Height and spread 10-20 cm (4-8 in).

Gazania hybrids

(South African daisy)
The eye-catching South African daisy has brilliantly colored flowers and some varieties have silvery foliage. It flowers profusely throughout the summer and excels in hot dry summers. Height 20-25 cm (8-10 in). Spread 30 cm (12 in).

Impatiens

(Busy Lizzie)
One of the most popular of all bedding plants, busy Lizzies will survive in partial shade as well as full sun. There are single- and double-flowered varieties. Probably the most popular are the New Guinea hybrids available in all shades of red through to pink and white. The variety Tango has orange flowers. Height and spread 23-30 cm (9-12 in).

Lobelia erinus

The traditional bedding plant for edges and the trailing varieties are used in hanging baskets. Most lobelias are blue but there are white and pink varieties. Height and spread of non-trailing varieties 4 in (10 cm).

Nemesia strumosa

Branching annual available in a large variety of colors, the flowers are 'two-lipped' and the lips are often in contrasting colors. The Carnival Series varieties are dwarf and very popular. Height 17-23 cm (7-9 in). Spread 10 cm (4 in).

Nicotiana

(Tobacco plant)
The modern hybrids are the most

commonly grown and are very popular. They are stockier, take up less room than the old varieties, flower during the day rather than just in the evening and are generally better plants – except that not all are fragrant and the old varieties have the most gorgeous scent that fills the air when the flowers open as dusk falls. Height (modern hybrids) 30-60 cm (1-2 ft). Spread 30-45 cm (12-18 in).

Petunia

One of the most popular bedding plants with large, funnel-shaped flowers in a wide variety of colors. They are often slightly scented. They do benefit from deadheading and are slightly prone to disease. Trailing varieties are available for hanging baskets. Height 23-30 cm (9-12 in). Spread 60 cm (2 ft).

Tagetes

(African and French marigolds) Nearly all marigolds are yellow or orange in color and they are excellent plants not only for summer bedding but to use as companion plants in the vegetable garden where they will deter flies and cabbage butterflies. These pests dislike the smell they give off. African marigolds are larger than French marigolds. Height (African marigolds) 30-90 cm (1-3 ft). Spread 25-45 cm (10-18 in).

Verbena x hybrida

There are many verbenas available. They all have small primrose-like flowers in groups at the end of short stalks. They are most attractive and come in many colors. 'Peaches and Cream' has pale orange-pink flowers that become cream-colored as they fade. Sandy Series comes in a number of vivid colors, red, pink, magenta and white with white eyes. Height 15-30 cm (6-12 in). Spread 30-60 cm (1-2 ft).

Below: *Petunia* **'Vogue'. Petunias are probably the most popular of all annuals. If you can, deadhead them throughout the year to encourage new blooms.**

Below: *Calendula officinalis*, pot marigolds, flower from midsummer onwards. They were much used in herbal medicine in the Middle Ages.

Opposite: *Eschscholzia californica*, Californian poppies, are among the easiest of all annuals to grow. They like a sunny site and come in many colors.

Hardy annuals can either be bought in a tray from a nursery and planted out or they can be sown directly into the ground where they are to flower. Sow several varieties at the same time and mark out patches with a stick so that the different flowers intermingle when they bloom.

Alyssum maritimum
(Sweet alyssum)
Mounds of small, white, honey-scented flowers, some varieties are lavender, pink or violet. Alyssum flowers from summer to early fall and is often grown as a drift or floral carpet. Height 10-13 cm (4-5 in). Spread 15 cm (6 in).

Calendula
(Pot marigold)
One of the traditional easy-to-grow cottage garden plants that bears yellow or orange flowers from mid-spring until the fall, it is often grown as a cut flower and was formerly used in herbal medicine. Dwarf varieties are available that can be grown as edging plants. Height 30-60 cm (1-2 ft). Spread 23-30 cm (9-12 in).

Eschscholzia
(California poppy)
One of the easiest of all annuals to grow, if you sprinkle some seed over bare ground in the fall or spring you will have flowers from summer to the fall. Californian poppies are usually yellow or orange but other colors are available. Self-seeds freely. Height 30 cm (1 ft). Spread 23 cm (9 in).

Iberis
(Candytuft)
For most gardeners iberis mean a dome of white, fragrant flowers that last from spring to the fall. However *I. umbellata* Fairy Series has pink, lilac-purple and red-pink flowers while the aptly named Flash Series is more colorful and has flowers in pink, purple or carmine-red. Height 15-30 cm (6-9 in). Spread 23 cm (9 in).

Limnanthes douglasii
(Poached-egg plant)
The poached-egg plant is a pretty annual that can be grown as ground cover and attracts bees and butterflies. Its petals are bright yellow in the center with white outer edges. It grows quickly and self-seeds freely. Height 15 cm (6 in). Spread 23 cm (9 in).

Malcolmia
(Virginia stock)
This is the most attractive little flower but has to be grown from seed. This should be sown in open ground throughout spring. It has sweetly scented red to purple flowers. The Compacta Series has varieties in white through to red and purple. Height 20 cm (8 in). Spread 12-15 cm (4-6 in).

PERENNIALS

The lazy gardener is best to avoid the large-scale herbaceous border. If you find yourself with a garden that has a large border there are two sensible courses of action open to you. The first, if it will not destroy the design of the garden, is to grass the border over and just add it to the lawn. Get someone to dig up all the plants, apply a systemic weedkiller to the area and leave it for some weeks. Then buy new topsoil to bring the level up to the surrounding lawn, level it, let the new soil settle, then sow grass seed. Unless you know precisely what you are doing and have the time to implement this strategy, it might be advisable to enlist some professional help over this.

The other course of action is to employ a gardener to help.

If you cannot do either of these then you will have to learn how to tackle the border. This, in itself, is perfectly simple but does require a number of hours each year.

If you have a small mixed border of shrubs and bulbs in a small garden then you could consider adding some favorite perennials. They are easy to maintain and they can provide color at times of the year when the shrubs and flowering trees are over.

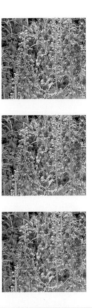

Left: *Delphinium* **'Carl Topping'.**

Below: *Alchemilla mollis*, Lady's mantle, makes a charming edge to a border with its soft green foliage and yellow flowers.

Right: *Aster novae-angliae* 'Barr's Pink'. New England asters flower from late summer through to the fall.

Opposite: Aquilegias flower in late spring and are available in many colors. They self-seed freely.

Perennials are plants that flower each year, mainly dying down in the winter although a few are evergreen and retain their leaves over winter. They all re-emerge next spring to flower. Most perennials don't live for ever and all grow bigger and bigger, if not in height then in width and spread. The most vigorous have a nasty habit of swamping their less sturdy neighbors and all gardeners have to be vigilant about digging out and throwing away surplus plants (or passing them on to fellow gardeners).

This is the main problem with perennials. They really have to be controlled. You may think that you have a well-spaced border with adequate room in the spring only to find in midsummer that everything is congested and the later shrubs and plants overwhelmed. The other main problem that is more pronounced if you have a traditional herbaceous border is that the plants have to be staked. The best way of doing this is to construct a frame of posts and then attach a strong, large-squared net so that the plants can grow through the netting. Then next spring as new growth starts get two strong men and pull all the old growth away with the net. Clean the net and you can start again.

Alcea
(Hollyhock)

Most hollyhocks are actually biennials although most gardeners treat them as short-lived perennials. They are tall plants and have colorful spikes of flowers in many colors from early-midsummer onwards. They are prone to rust and prefer full sun. Plant at the back of the border or in the center of a two-sided border.

Alchemilla
(Lady's mantle)

A large genus of plants, the most commonly grown form is *A. mollis*, a plant that provokes strong reactions from many gardeners. It is very vigorous and invasive and while some love its soft green foliage and delicate yellow flowers, others have been known to spray it with weedkiller to remove it. Flowers from midsummer onwards.

Anthemis tinctoria

(Ox-eye chamomile, Golden marguerite)

Daisy-like yellow flowers with a pronounced darker center typical of all daisies, and feathery green foliage. They are not very long-lived and should be cut back hard after flowering to promote growth from the base. There is a number of varieties. They flower from midsummer onwards.

Aquilegia

(Columbine)

One of the favorite spring-flowering border plants, that has the merit (or demerit) of self-seeding freely. They require little maintenance. They have delightful, delicate-looking flowers, ranging from deep purple, almost black, through pink and yellow to clear white and there is a number of hybrids and varieties available. The old cottage garden favorite, *A. vulgaris*, Granny's bonnets, and its varieties, is still one of the best.

Aster

(Michaelmas daisy)

Popular hardy herbaceous perennials that start flowering in early fall. They are tolerant of most garden conditions. The commonest garden Michaelmas daisies are *A. novae-angliae* and *A. novi-belgii* and their varieties. The plants are available in a wide range of colors from blue, purple, and yellow, to pink and white.

Campanula

(Bellflower)

There is a large number of campanulas ranging from large and medium-sized border plants, *C. latifolia* can grow to 1.5 m (5 ft) to the creeping *C. carpatica* that is most useful as a ground-cover plant. They have distinctive blue, white or violet flowers, shaped like bells. Tall border varieties will need staking. They prefer some shade and grow in all soils except very wet and acid.

Delphinium

Delphiniums are one of the best-loved flowers of summer and add height and color to any herbaceous border. Delphiniums, traditionally, are blue, but they are available in a range of colors from white, pink, and yellow. All need staking and are best propagated by basal cuttings in early spring.

Dicentra

(Bleeding heart, Dutchman's trousers)

A favorite garden perennial that flowers early in the year. *D. spectabilis*, pink and white flowers, and *D. s.* f. *alba*, white flowers, are the two large varieties most generally found but *D. formosa* and *D.* 'Stuart Boothman' are much smaller with attractive grey-green foliage and charming pink flowers reminiscent of stalks of bell heather, they spread freely.

Digitalis

(Foxglove)

Imposing plants for the large herbaceous border, foxgloves are biennials that seed themselves freely. Some gardeners will not tolerate them on this account. The most commonly grown are the *D. purpurea* Excelsior Hybrids that carry long spikes of flowers, white, pink or purple. The seeds are poisonous.

Eryngium

(Sea holly)

Useful and attractive garden perennials, the two varieties most commonly grown are *E. bourgatii*, bluish purple flowerheads, and *E. giganteum*, Miss Willmott's ghost, a startling plant especially seen in the late evening that has pale blue flowerheads surrounded by silver white bracts.

Euphorbia

A large and varied genus of plants. The most common garden varieties are *E. characias* ssp. *wulfenii*, a magnificent plant if you have a large enough garden to accommodate it, and *E. amygdaloides* and *E. cyparissias*, that can be grown in smaller borders. The large-flowered varieties prefer full sun. The sap is an irritant and care must be taken when handling the plants.

Geranium

(Cranesbill)

Not to be confused with pelargoniums, geraniums are a large genus of hardy perennials that no garden should be without. There is a number of outstanding varieties that flower throughout the summer; among the most popular are *G.* 'Johnson's Blue', violet-blue flowers, *G. endressii* and *G.* x *oxonianum* 'Claridge Druce', pink flowers and *G. clarkei* 'Kashmir White', white.

Helleborus

(Hellebore, Christmas rose, Lenten rose)

Hellebores are one of the joys of the winter garden. The best-known species is *H. niger*, the Christmas rose, with its white flowers, greenish centers and yellow stamens, *H. orientalis*, the Lenten rose, has purple, pink or grey flowers and both *H. argutifolius* syn. *H. corsicus*, the Corsican hellebore, and *H. foetidus*, the stinking hellebore, have green flowers. They prefer, indeed need, some shade.

Lupinus

(Lupin)

Herbaceous border favorites that have been popular plants for many years. The majority of the lupins grown are Russell hybrids that form substantial clumps and carry large spikes of flowers in many colors. Lupins are somewhat prone to pests and disease and are best renewed every four years or so, to save money raise some plants from seed. They are poisonous and should be avoided if small children use the garden.

**Opposite: Purple foxglove
(Digitalis purpurea).**

**Left: Almost all the lupins
grown in gardens belong to
the group Russell Hybrids,
available in a large variety
of colors.**

Nepeta
(Catmint)
One of the easiest and commonest of all the perennials, catmint is an excellent plant for the front of the border. It is low-growing and carries a mass of pale blue flowers on spreading stems. Cut back at the end of the summer and divide in spring. 'Six Hills Giant' is the most commonly grown variety.

Osteospermum
Popular garden subshrubs and perennials that are grown for their daisy-like flowers. They are not fully hardy and in the colder parts of the country are best grown as annuals. Varieties come in a number of colors, yellow, white, purple and pink. 'Whirligig' has the most extraordinary shaped flowerhead.

Paeonia
(Peony, peony rose)
Peonies are excellent plants for the mixed border and are often long-lived but they resent being moved and can take time to become established. There are two forms, the garden perennial, and the upright deciduous shrub, the tree peony. The flowers, often double or semi-double, are generally red, pink or white, although there are yellow varieties. The most attractively named peony is *P. mlokosewitschii*, popularly called Molly-the-Witch, that has single yellow flowers. *P. suffruticosa* and its varieties, is the best-known tree peony with spectacular flowers, sometimes as large as 25 cm (10 in) across.

Penstemon
A deservedly popular genus of evergreen, or semi-evergreen, garden perennials grown for their long spikes of tubular, bell-shaped flowers in colors ranging from deep red through to pale pink and white. Among the most attractive are *P.* 'Andenken an Friedrich Hahn', that used to be known as 'Garnet', deep red flowers, 'Apple Blossom', pink and white, and 'White Bedder', white, tinged with pink as it ages.

Phlox
A diverse genus of perennials, the most commonly grown are the *P. paniculata* varieties that carry large flowers grouped on conical heads. Among the best are 'Amethyst', violet, 'Fujiyama', white and 'Mother-of-Pearl', white with pink tints. *P. stolonifera*, creeping phlox, is low-growing and a good plant for the front of the border or a rock garden. It prefers acid soil.

Above: *Primula obconica*, one of the many varieties of primrose that is usually grown as an annual.

Opposite: *Viola* x *wittrockiana*, winter pansies, are one of the best garden flowers and can provide color all through the winter.

Some bedding plants take two years to flower, seeds are sown in the first year and the plants are then planted out in the position where they are to flower the following spring, in late summer to fall. These are biennials. There are some other bedding plants that will flower from year to year, they are perennials.

Bellis perennis
(Daisy)
Hardy biennial. Many varieties have been bred from the common daisy of most lawns, some so large and colorful that it appears they can hardly be related. The Tasso Series has double flowers 6 cm (2.5 in) across, Pomponette Series has smaller flowers 4 cm (1.5 in) across, while the popular Roggli Series has semi-double flowers slightly smaller. All have flowers in white and various shades of pink to red. Height and spread 5-20 cm (2-8 in) depending on the series grown.

Dianthus barbatus
(Sweet William)
One of the best-loved cottage garden plants usually grown as a biennial. It has large flowerheads usually in shades of pink and red sometimes edged with white. It is sweetly scented. They prefer a dry position and alkaline soil. Height 25-45 cm (10-18 in). Spread 23-30 cm (9-12 in).

Diascia cordata
A lesser known, mat-forming, perennial that carries open pink flowers held up on lax stems from summer to fall. Height 15 cm (6 in). Spread 50 cm (20 in).

Erysimum cheiri
(Wallflower)
You may well find this listed in catalogues under its former name of cheiranthus, the two have been merged. Wallflowers are popular cottage garden plants, very sweet scented, with mainly bronze, dusky orange, red or yellow flowers although some paler varieties can be grown. Many are short-lived perennials but they are more successful when grown as biennials. Height 30-45 cm (1-1.5 ft). Spread 23-30 cm (9-12 in).

Primula
(Polyanthus, Primrose)
There is a vast number of primulas. For the purposes of bedding plants primulas are split into two groups although this distinction can become blurred.

The Primrose Group is grown as a hardy perennial outside and flowers in spring. One of the most attractive is still the original species plant, *P. vulgaris*, with its pale yellow, slightly fragrant flowers. Varieties are available in many colors.

The second group is the Polyanthus Group, grown from summer-sown seed and planted out

in the fall to flower through the winter and the following spring. These winter-flowering primulas are excellent plants and add welcome color to the garden in the depths of winter. Height 12-20 cm (4-8 in). Spread 20-35 cm (8-14 in).

Viola x wittrockiana
(Violas, Pansies)
Really worthwhile plants, there are so many varieties available that a selection can be grown that will be in flower all year round – the winter-flowering pansies are justifiably particularly popular. They are available in many bright colors, purple, yellow, white and orange, and many flowers have strongly marked centers rather like small cheerful faces painted on the flowers. The lazy gardener can plant out some any time to add color to tubs or borders. Height 15-23 cm (6-9 in). Spread 15 cm (6 in).

The lazy gardener does not want to spend a great deal of time weeding. One of the best ways to avoid a large crop of weeds is to grow ground-cover plants that cover the soil and exclude annual weeds. Many of the most vigorous perennial plants do this automatically, particularly as they age and become established, other plants are specifically grown as ground cover.

TIPS

FOR THE *lazy* GARDENER

81

Left: *Stachys byzantina* **'Silver Carpet', syn.** *S. lanata* **'Silver Carpet', a ground-cover plant grown for its silver foliage only. It does not flower.**

Below: *Pulmonaria saccharata*, lungwort, is one of the delights of spring with its spotted leaves and pink and blue flowers.

Opposite: *Vinca major*, greater periwinkle.

Ajuga
(Bugle)

A. reptans is one of the most decorative of the small ground-cover plants and spreads freely. It likes fertile moist soil and some shade. Among the most popular varieties are 'Atropurpurea', deep bronze-purple leaves, 'Braunherz', deep bronze leaves, 'Burgundy Glow', silvery-green leaves with red markings, and 'Catlin's Giant', large dark purple leaves. All have attractive erect spikes of blue flowers.

Bergenia
(Elephant's ears)

These useful plants, which rejoice in their descriptive common name, flower in early spring and generally have upright clusters of pink to purple flowers. Some varieties are white. The large round leaves often turn brilliant red in the fall and they are good ground-cover plants for borders and the wilder areas of the garden.

Corydalis
(Fumitory)

Attractive, vigorous, ground-cover perennial with delicate fern-like, green leaves and long tubular flowers that last for several weeks. The best species are *C. flexuosa*, blue flowers, *C. lutea*, yellow, and *C. solida*, red to pink.

Erigeron
(Fleabane)

E. karvinskianus is often found growing down walls and on paving. It has small daisy-like flowers, that open white and then turn to pink and purple as they age.

Hedera colchica
(Persian ivy)

A vigorous ivy that works well as a ground-cover plant. It will also cover walls and trees. The two varieties to grow are 'Dentata' with bright green leaves and 'Dentata Variegata', light green leaves with creamy margins.

Lamium maculatum
(Dead nettle)

The dead nettle can make an attractive plant and is good ground cover. There is a number of varieties, 'Aureum' has gold leaves with white centers and pink flowers, 'Beacon Silver' silver leaves and pink flowers, 'White Nancy' has white flowers and silver leaves with narrow green margins. They are not so vigorous as the species plant. All dead nettles grow best in shade.

Myosotis
(Forget-me-not)

The forget-me-not may be a humble plant but it is brilliantly invasive and can be used with great effect to carpet a rose bed with its blue flowers or fill in a corner in a herbaceous border. The alpine forms, *M. alpestris*, are the most compact.

Pachysandra terminalis

One of the best plants to grow as ground cover in shade, this evergreen subshrub has dark green leaves and small white flowers in late spring.

Pulmonaria
(Lungwort)

These are among the earliest plants to flower in spring. The flowers are funnel-shaped and held on upright stems, usually pink or shades of blue, although some white varieties are available. Lungworts get their common name from their spotted leaves and make good ground-cover plants. They like some shade.

Stachys
(Betony)

One of the best ground-cover plants in the garden. This is quite a large genus but few are worth cultivating: the best-known are *S. byzantina*, lamb's ears or loppylugs, that has intensely silver, white, felted leaves and small pink flowers in summer and *S. b.* 'Silver Carpet' with silver leaves. This variety does not flower and is grown entirely for its foliage.

Veronica prostrata
(Creeping speedwell)

A number of speedwells make good ground-cover plants. *V. prostrata* is a dense mat-forming plant that has spikes of blue flowers in early summer, the varieties 'Spode Blue' has brighter blue flowers and 'Trehane' has golden-yellow leaves and deep blue flowers. They prefer full sun or partial shade and well-drained soil. They are good plants for the front of a mixed border.

Vinca major and V. minor
(Periwinkle)

Periwinkles are really mat-forming evergreen shrubs rather than perennials. They carry mainly purple or blue flowers from spring through to the fall and make excellent ground cover. They do not like very dry conditions but apart from that tolerate any soil and grow best in partial sun.

BULBS

For many, bulbs are the epitome of instant gardening. They are excellent plants for the lazy gardener. They provide instant color and once they are in position they can virtually be ignored until the time comes to admire them the following season.

There are three rules, one a counsel of perfection, two seriously important.

1 Check the conditions that you can offer your bulbs, a number grow best when they are planted in light shade and nearly all like well-drained soil. Some however need sun. Try and give the bulbs the conditions that they prefer.

2 The second, most important rule for growing bulbs successfully is to let all the foliage die right down before cutting the grass or tidying up the old foliage if the bulbs are grown in a bed. This really is very important. If you don't do it, for the sake of tidiness or whatever, then you won't have many flowers the following year. Bulbs build up their strength through the nourishment they receive from their leaves. A feed applied to all bulbs when they are in leaf is well worth the trouble.

3 Plant properly. This means planting all bulbs a good deal deeper than you might imagine, two and a half times the height of the bulb is a good average. One of the main causes of 'blindness' – no flowers on daffodils – is because they were not planted deeply enough in the first place.

For the lazy gardener certain of the best known and best loved bulbs have to be excluded as they really should be lifted each year when they have finished flowering and then planted out again in the fall. These include tulips, gladioli and hyacinths, although many people leave hyacinths in the ground year after year. Also snowdrops really should have their clumps split each year. This increases the stock. They are best grown in a wild area of the garden if you have one available.

85

Left: Narcissi 'Peeping Tom'.

Below: *Eranthis hyemalis*, winter aconite, one of the earliest spring flowers that often emerges with the snowdrops.

Opposite: *Chionodoxa luciliae*, glory of the snow, is less well known that it should be. The bulbs colonize freely once established.

86

Every gardener, even the laziest, knows the common bulbs of spring, daffodils, narcissus, snowdrops, crocuses and bluebells. There is a number of other bulbs that can be planted and are well worth making room for in the garden, in addition to the old favorites.

Anemone

Anemones are a large genus that contains both spring and fall-flowering plants. The favorite spring anemones are varieties of the tuberous species, *A. blanda* and *A. coronaria*. They have colorful red, white or blue flowers with attractive, green, deeply divided leaves.

Chionodoxa

(Glory of the snow)

One of the lesser-known bulbs of spring that deserves to be more widely planted. Chionodoxa have delicate star-shaped flowers, generally in shades of blue although some are pink. They self-seed freely.

Convallaria

(Lily-of-the-Valley)

A classic garden plant that may be difficult to establish. It likes shade and moist soil and if the bulbs are happy with their lot they spread freely and produce sprays of deliciously scented white flowers in late spring. *C. majalis* var. *rosea* has pink flowers.

Eranthis hyemalis

(Winter aconite)

Winter aconites are tubers that prefer alkaline soil that does not dry out in summer. Given these conditions they will colonize freely. They flower with snowdrops and are often grown together in semi-woodland, where the carpets of the small yellow and white flowers are particularly attractive in the early months of the year.

Leucojum vernum

(Snowflake)

Just like giant snowdrops, some species of snowflakes flower in summer and the fall, but *L. vernum*, the spring snowflake, and its varieties flower in spring. They have charming, bell-shaped, green-tipped flowers.

Scilla siberica

(Siberian squill)

One of the prettiest of all the spring bulbs with dainty blue heads rather like blue snowdrops although each flower stalk may carry up to five flowers. They like to grow in full sun.

Above: *Agapanthus* **Headbourne Hybrids provide beautiful flowers in late summer.**

Opposite: *Allium giganteum*, **ornamental onion, planted in a gravel bed in a dry garden. They tolerate dry conditions well.**

Bulbs do not just flower in spring, There is a number that flower in the summer. They are generally planted in the herbaceous border and while some require staking they are easy plants once established.

Agapanthus
(African lily)
These beautiful bulbs are not fully hardy and need protection in colder parts of the country. Where they flourish they eventually make a massed display of blue or white flowers according to the variety grown. Headbourne Hybrids are generally hardier that the species plants. They like full sun and shelter and also grow well in containers.

Allium
(Ornamental onion)
Excellent summer-flowering bulbs available in a variety of colors from pink, blue, white and yellow. *A. giganteum* is a seriously large plant that can grow as high as 2 m (6 ft) when it is grown in the right conditions, others can be much, much smaller. They all like full sun.

Colchicum
(Meadow saffron)
Charming bulbs that flower in the fall and are often, wrongly, referred to as fall crocus. *C. autumnale*, has crocus-like pink flowers in the fall, other varieties are deeper pink, yellow or white. The leaves appear after the flowers and last until midsummer.

Eremurus
(Foxtail lily, King's spear)
Another spectacular garden perennial with long single spikes of flowers. They flower best in a sheltered position and prefer slightly acid soil. *E. himalaicus* bears white flowers and *E. robustus*, pink. They need staking and have to be grown in well-drained, rich soil in full sun to give of their best.

Lilium regale
(Regal lily)
There are huge numbers of lilies in many shapes and sizes but the Regal lily is among the best known. They are well worth growing in any garden for their exceptionally fragrant trumpet-shaped white flowers that appear in midsummer. Regal lilies will grow in nearly all soils except very alkaline ones and they also do well in tubs on patios. They prefer full sun. The only drawback for the lazy gardener is that they do need staking.

Nerine bowdenii
(Guernsey lily)
Bulbous perennials that have decorative sprays of pink flowers in the fall. They used to be considered greenhouse plants only but they are perfectly hardy given the protection of a south or south-west-facing wall. They prefer sandy soil.

VEGETABLES

Vegetables are not really for the lazy gardener. They are a lot of work, not just in cultivating the soil and planting, but tending them throughout the year, weeding between the rows, thinning the crops, netting them against attacks by pigeons and other birds, guarding them from slugs, and, if you grow brassicas, guarding them, as best you can, from the caterpillars of the cabbage white butterfly.

Left: *Beta vulgaris*, **beetroot.**

On the other hand you might just enjoy the feeling of pride and achievement that comes from harvesting delicious vegetables that you have grown yourself, in which case you are well on the way to being a lazy gardener no longer. If you are tempted to try and grow vegetables you do not need a vast vegetable garden, a small plot, say 3 x 5 m (9 x 16 ft) will provide far more than you think.

If you want to grow some, concentrate on those vegetables that taste about 350% better when you have grown and picked them, than they ever would bought from the local supermarket. The other main bonus is that you know they are organic and chemical free and not sprayed countless times to produce them looking perfect and tasting of little for the supermarket shelves.

You can do certain things that make growing vegetables a great deal easier. The main thing is to abandon digging almost entirely. When a crop has finished fork over the soil very lightly, pull out the annual weeds and then, if you have it, spread a thick layer of garden compost over the surface. When you come to plant broccoli or other brassicas, lay a double layer of newspaper on the soil, cover this with another layer of compost and then cut through the newspaper with a knife and plant into the compost beneath.

You can go a long way to eliminate weeds from the kitchen garden by adopting the technique of putting down newspaper and spreading compost on top. If you want you can lay sheets of plastic but newspaper has the advantage of being porous and you will find that at the end of the year it has rotted away and the compost has been absorbed into the soil, thus providing a more fertile growing medium. This is particularly useful if you garden on heavy clay.

VEGETABLES

Below: Carrots ready to pull and store.

Opposite: Harvest time: the reward for the gardener who chooses to grow vegetables.

VEGETABLES GROWING THROUGH THE WINTER
Fava beans
Plant them in mid-late fall if your climate is reasonably mild or early in spring the following year. Harvest from late spring onwards. Pinch out the tops when the first flowers have formed. This makes bushier plants and helps to prevent infestations by blackfly. The tall varieties will need some support. Dwarf varieties are available for the smaller garden.

Broccoli
It is well worth growing three or four plants of purple or green sprouting broccoli. Plant them out in summer and the early varieties will be ready for picking from late winter onwards. They supply a long succession of spears. They will need room and protection from caterpillars and birds over the winter.

Perpetual beet, Swiss chard, Rhubarb chard
Sow these vegetables in the spring and you can go on picking them from summer and for the next 11-12 months. Young leaves taste best. The connoisseur will tell you that they don't taste quite as good as spinach but they are excellent value.

REALLY GOOD SUMMER VEGETABLES
Beetroot
A vastly underrated vegetable. Small beetroot cooked and served hot with butter and garlic is a dish for the Gods. Sow spring-early summer when all danger of frost has passed and harvest summer to fall. They should be thinned.

Carrots
A vegetable that tastes so much better than anything you can ever buy in a shop. Sow in spring and early summer and harvest midsummer-fall. It is worth growing small rows, sowing every two weeks, to produce a succession of crops. They require thinning.

French beans
Sow when all danger of frost has passed or under cloches in spring. Harvest from summer onwards. They may need some support.

Peas
Difficult to grow successfully, they are beloved of the birds and the seeds must be protected otherwise you won't get a crop at all. The snow pea varieties, such as Sugar Snap, where the whole pod is eaten are simply delicious. They require support of wire, pea sticks or netting up which they can climb.

Potatoes
These are hard work to grow but if you like new potatoes it is worth growing a few of the best first earlies because they taste so much better than anything you can buy

in the shops. There are methods of growing them in piles of old tyres but this is probably more trouble than digging the traditional trench.

String beans

Grow them up a tripod made from bamboo canes and they take up little room in the garden. Plant two seeds at the foot of each pole when all danger of frost has passed, remove one if both germinate. Spray the flowers with water lightly in the summer as this aids pollination. If you have too many, freeze the excess.

Other vegetables that are quite easy to grow if you think it worthwhile and have the room are: leeks; onions; zucchini (best grown on a mound of compost); turnips; rutabagas.

Barely worthwhile as they take up a good deal of room: the brassicas (cabbage; brussels sprouts, calabrese; cauliflower – cauliflowers are difficult to grow successfully without a good deal of care and attention).

Other difficult vegetables might include: parsnips (they take ages to germinate), celery; endive; sweetcorn, grow it in a square, not rows, (it needs to be pretty hot in the summer for them to grow successfully and grey squirrels are particularly fond of them, if my experience is anything to go by).

HERBS

Herbs are not really something for the lazy gardener but if there is pressure from the cook then a number of good herbs are reasonably easy to grow.

Herbs fall into two categories; those that flourish in the normal climate of this country and those that come from the Mediterranean, and need warmth and protection in hard winters. Some herbs are perennials, some shrubs, and some are grown as annuals.

HERBS THAT YOU MIGHT CONSIDER GROWING

Basil
Grow as an annual. Sow seed under glass and plant out when all danger of frosts has passed. Needs full sun and rich, moist soil.

Bay
Buy a tree (*Laurus nobilis*) and grow it in a tub or in a sunny place in the garden; as it grows move it into larger pots, pick leaves as you need them.

Chives
A small perennial bulb, a member of the onion family (*allium*). Divide clumps in the spring if you want to increase your stock.

Cilantro
An annual. Sow seed in the fall or spring. Thin the rows. Likes full sun and neutral to acid soil.

Mint
A spreading perennial much used in the kitchen. Very invasive. Remove the bottom from a bucket, sink it into the ground and plant mint inside the rim. There is a number of varieties available. Prefers moist, fertile, well-drained soil and some shade.

Parsley
A short-lived perennial, often grown as an annual. Sow seed in spring. Don't give up hope the seed takes a long time to germinate.

Rosemary
Evergreen, upright shrub that may need some protection in really hard winters. It likes sun and fairly poor, well-drained soil.

Sage
Evergreen, perennial or subshrub. It likes rich, well-drained soil, full sun and some shelter. Divide plants in spring.

Thyme
Bushy, evergreen, spreading subshrub. Likes well-drained alkaline soil and full sun. Clip after flowering.

GREENHOUSE

The lazy gardener does not have a greenhouse. They are time-consuming and encourage the gardener to grow large numbers of plants from seed, propagate a number of house plants, overwinter pelargoniums, store dahlias, gladioli, gloxinia and begonia tubers, grow indoor tomatoes, eggplants and cucumbers and dabble with growing chrysanthemums. They need shading in summer and cleaning before the winter. They also need ventilation and careful control of pests and diseases. If you do happen to have a greenhouse and you are a truly lazy gardener then the only thing to do is to use it for storage space.

INDEX

Figures in italic indicate Illustrations

Photography © Collins and Brown

All photographs Collins and Brown except; wheelbarrow and shears on jacket, pages 8 (tl), 9 (br), 13 (br), 15 (br), 21 (br), 23 (br), 24 (bl), 26, 27, 54 (bl), 90, 91, 95 supplied by PhotoDisc